Lost and Found Lovers

Lost and Found Lovers

FACTS AND FANTASIES
OF REKINDLED ROMANCES

NANCY KALISH, PH.D.

WILLIAM MORROW AND COMPANY, INC.

NEW YORK

It is the policy of William Morrow and Company, Inc., and its imprints and affiliates, recognizing
the importance of preserving what has been written, to print the books we publish on acid-free
paper, and we exert our best efforts to that end.

Library of Congress Cataloging-in-Publication Data
Kalish, Nancy.
Lost and found lovers : facts and fantasies of rekindled romances
/ Nancy Kalish.
p.   cm.
Includes bibliographical references and index.
ISBN 0-688-15181-7
1. Man-woman relationships.   2. Reunions.   I. Title.
HQ801.K32   1997

306.7—dc20   96-34679

CIP

Printed in the United States of America
First Edition

1 2 3 4 5 6 7 8 9 10

BOOK DESIGN BY LEAH LOCOCO

TO MY PARENTS,
JOSEPH AND DOROTHY KALISH,
WHO TAUGHT ME ABOUT LOVE
BY EXAMPLE

ACKNOWLEDGMENTS

NO WORK IS SOLELY a product of one creator. Perhaps this is especially true for research studies that rely on numerous volunteers. So I am first and foremost indebted to all the participants of the Lost Love Project, who freely gave me their time and trust by filling out questionnaires and telling their stories. All participants will remain anonymous and receive no credit other than this note, but I can tell them here how much I appreciate their help.

I am grateful to the many talented journalists, television and radio producers, hosts, and anchors who publicized my research and its need for volunteers. I might never have been able to find so many participants without them.

Thanks to California State University, Sacramento, and the Department of Psychology for support. I am appreciative of the guidance I received from the Institute for Social Research and from its Director, Dr. Carole Barnes, who nurtured the questionnaire design and initial data entry.

Several students worked on an ongoing basis on this project: graduate students Michael Billard and Patrick Nooren with data encoding and computer analyses, and undergraduates Carole McKindley, Christina Shoberg, Chelly Barnes, and Dolly Eyaw-Bourne with the mailing of results and developing a data base of volunteers for future research. These tasks were sometimes tedious, and I am grateful to these students for their dedication and hard work.

Thanks also to friends from Brandeis University, class of 1995, and to friends in Sacramento and New Jersey, who contributed to Chapter Three and generally encouraged my efforts. Joe Baltake, movie critic for *The Sacramento Bee,* provided me with valuable suggestions about rekindled love films.

Ideally, an editor should bring out the best in a manuscript and leave an author happier with its pages than before. By these standards, I was fortunate to have had *two* of the best: Julie Olfe of Julian, California, and Toni Sciarra of William Morrow.

I was also lucky to have had two terrific literary agents. Nikki Smith and

Eleanore Lee of Smith/Skolnik Literary Management provided comfort and cheer along with their very competent agenting.

My gratitude to my mother and father is endless. And to my daughter Robin: Thank you for your help and patience during the course of this project—and for your lifelong lovingkindness.

CONTENTS

Lost and Found Lovers

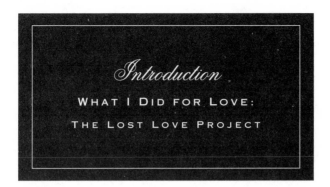

I BEGAN THE LOST Love Project several months after I reestablished contact with my college boyfriend, because I wanted to learn more about rekindled romance. I had read Robert James Waller's *The Bridges of Madison County* and had cried over the lost love of Francesca Johnson and Robert Kincaid. But I wondered what would have happened if the photographer and the Iowa housewife had managed to meet again years later. Would their former passion have continued as true love? What do *real people* experience when they reconnect years later with a Lost Lover?

I had no idea how many people I could expect to attract to my study, and not many ideas about how to find them. The Lost Love Project started slowly as a small study of rekindlers in the Sacramento and San Francisco areas. But after a few months, it caught the attention of the media. Then people from all over the world began to find *me*. Within two years, my little snowball of a project had turned into an avalanche of questionnaires, stories, faxes, e-mail, and telephone messages. I was having so much fun with the research that I became a little obsessed. Here is how it all began.

THE SEARCH

Uncovering a hidden population of rekindled couples wasn't easy. My first challenge was to design the questionnaire. The questions came from my own Lost and Found Love experience, from listening to others who had rekindled romances, and from the fictitious situations I had read about in some of the books and plays discussed in Chapter Three. I chose five years as the minimum separation time for the couples to qualify for this study. Five years seemed long enough to make sure that there really had been an emotional and physical split, and for the lovers to have experienced some growth (even other romances) between their first and later connections.

After four questionnaire revisions, a pilot study, and approval from the California State University at Sacramento, Human Subjects Committee, I was ready to go. I included a cover sheet of introduction, a follow-up form for people who wanted to receive results, and a stamped, self-addressed envelope in each package I sent out. I rented a post office box and ran a paid, two-inch display ad in *The Sacramento Bee*. I used the same wording for all requests for participation throughout the project:

COLLEGE RESEARCHER SEEKS PEOPLE WHO LOVED SOMEONE YEARS AGO, PARTED, THEN 5 OR MORE YEARS LATER TRIED ANOTHER RELATIONSHIP WITH THAT PERSON. FOR AN ANONYMOUS QUESTIONNAIRE, SEND A MAILING ADDRESS TO: THE LOST LOVE PROJECT, P.O. BOX 19692, SACRAMENTO, CA 95819.

The two-day ad brought in only eleven participants. I tried a newspaper with an even larger circulation, the *San Francisco Chronicle,* but that brought in only two responses.

I went into high gear. I called a local radio station, KFBK, and suggested that my project would make a good Valentine's Day story. This landed me on a popular talk show, *The Tom Sullivan Show,* where I spoke with callers who had rekindled a romance, or thought about a "special someone" from their past. Mentioning the Lost Love Project post office box on the air brought in twenty participants. A year later, I was invited back to discuss my preliminary results, and more respondents entered the Lost Love Project.

I decided to make the Lost Love Project national, even though I had first envisioned it as a California study. I called every radio station and newspaper that was listed in a directory of toll-free telephone numbers. I explained my project and asked if I might send them a brief announcement to read on the air or to print in the paper. Some wrote feature stories about my Lost Love experience and research.

Sometimes the respondents themselves helped me find others. My New Zealand connection owes its existence to one supportive woman, now married to her Lost and Found Lover and living in Arizona:

WE WERE SEPARATED BY WARTIME circumstances. We were engaged in 1943 when I was a New Zealand teenager and he was a U.S. Marine. But our romance was disrupted when he was posted elsewhere and by a long break in our correspondence. I became engaged to someone else, and *then* I received a bundle of letters that he had written all along but that never arrived. We went on to marry other people.

My Lost Lover became a widower, and I was divorced. We reestablished contact through his aunt and continued with a series of letters and long distance telephone calls. When I met him again in Los Angeles, we just stood and hugged each other for awhile. It was terrific. Nine days later, we married.

We have been very happy for fifteen years. There certainly didn't seem to be a gap of thirty-eight years. We never cease to marvel at the miracle of coming together after so long, though it only seemed like a week or two.

She took the time to send me newspaper clippings about her own story, stories about other New Zealand World War II rekindled romances, and names and addresses of people in New Zealand who might help me further. They did. Soon an article about my quest appeared in a newspaper there, and *voilà,* I had an international project!

Other people sent clippings from their local newspapers about couples who had rekindled romances after many years apart. I called Directory Assistance and obtained telephone numbers for these sweethearts in most cases. When I could not obtain a telephone number directly for one couple in their eighties, I called the church mentioned in the article. Sometimes television talk shows had guests who had renewed romances. I called them, too.

By this time the study was eight months old, and I had become a driven woman. I loved receiving people's fascinating stories and watching my bank of data grow. People from all over the world took the time to fill out a questionnaire or to help me in other ways. Without all these generous helpers, there would be no Lost Love Project.

As I struggled to find participants, my mother suggested that I watch *Leeza*. She thought it was a sensible talk show that might be interested in my topic and allow me to recruit some people from the audience. Because I had been granted a sabbatical leave to pursue my research, I was at home in the mornings. The first time I watched *Leeza,* I listened with near-disbelief as a voice-over requested people who had rekindled a romance with a high school sweetheart, or wanted to, to contact the show for an upcoming episode. What an incredible coincidence! I ran for a pencil, scribbled the toll-free number, and called immediately to tell them about my Lost Love Project.

Four days later, Paramount flew me to Burbank to appear on the show. I found it difficult to return to the routine of the classroom after my fifteen minutes of fame (rerun two months later for an additional fifteen minutes). Most important, I was thrilled to have succeeded in my original intent—to find survey participants. The moral of this story: Always listen to your mother.

My Lost Love Project was taking on a life of its own. A visiting professor took one of my public service announcements back to England and sent it to several newspapers there. Some of my students sent questionnaires to relatives, friends, and newspapers in Ecuador, Malaysia, Poland, and Tonga. How a story about my research wound up in the Punjab press, I still do not know. I also had good success finding Lost and Found Lovers with my cyber-postings on the information superhighways. The Internet proved especially useful for collecting international data and attracting a young population.

One January day, I had the best idea yet for finding Lost and Found Lovers. I remembered my success with the Valentine's Day radio show the previous year, so I telephoned the local office of the Associated Press to ask them if they wanted to write a story about my project for Valentine's Day. The AP liked my idea and the story was assigned to John Howard. It did not, however, get printed for Valentine's Day. California had some weather catastrophes that were more important than the Lost Love Project, and the story was left unfinished. Then one April morning, I was awakened at six A.M. by a call from a Chicago radio station that wanted to interview me: The AP "Valentine's Day" story had hit the wire services.

It is not an exaggeration to say that the press release changed my life. Five radio stations called later that day, and many more over the months to follow. I became accustomed to giving radio interviews over my home phone very early in the morning (because of time zone differences), then going back to sleep for a little while before work. Television networks followed suit and cameras followed me around the college.

Mail poured in. Lost and Found Lovers tracked me down through the university, through Directory Assistance, by calling radio stations or television studios. Now they seemed as driven to find me as I had been to find them!

Newspapers in Hong Kong, England, India, and China sent faxes to me at the university. Each new interview attracted more of the same. More than one hundred fifty letters flooded my mailbox. "Have one of your associates get back to us," one magazine suggested. I had to smile: I was the entire Lost Love Project, and everything was generated from my briefcase and laptop computer.

One magazine published only two lines about the research ("Great Job Titles of the Western World: Director of the Lost Love Project"), but still generated telephone calls from talk shows and movie studios. One movie producer told me, after he read my own rekindled romance story, that it would not make a good movie because the ending was too sad. Well, I didn't like that ending, either. But television news shows liked to use the Lost Love Project itself as a positive story.

One man used my research as a jumping-off point for a marriage proposal:

I READ ABOUT THE LOST Love Project in an AP wire article. It so happens that I have had a faithful infatuation for thirty years with a woman in another country, since college. I am planning to send her a copy of the article about you. Both of us were very shy in college, and we maintained an on-again off-again correspondence until a few years ago, in which neither she nor I expressed our true feelings toward each other.

Then a few years ago, I became ill with a series of mild but chronic medical problems which improved just three years ago. I re-contacted her with a high degree of self-esteem and confidence, and said that I was interested in marriage. I think she'd like to. The article might loosen her up.

One woman wrote to tell me that she and her Lost and Found Lover read parts of the AP article about the Lost Love Project along with the vows at their marriage ceremony. A reporter mentioned that her Lost Lover had recently contacted her after seeing a press release about my research, and they had begun dating again. I realized I was now *creating* Lost and Found Lovers, not just locating them!

A year went by without any letup in media interviews or responses from rekindlers. When Valentine's Day rolled around again, the Associated Press called *me*. Another article about the Lost Love Project was released—on Valentine's Day—by Malcolm Ritter. Three hundred letters poured in.

I also mentioned my research wherever my daily routines took me. I gave questionnaires to students, staff, and faculty at the university, a veterinary assistant, a physical therapist, receptionists in a tile store and a car body shop, people who noticed my posters as I stood in line to pay for copying them, a grocery store checker, fellow clients at a hair salon, seatmates on airplanes, a salesperson at a Sacramento clothing store, an antiquarian bookstore owner, two literary agents, the sister of a textbook representative, and many others. I learned to carry a questionnaire or two wherever I went. And so, over the course of two years, I found my population of Lost and Found Lovers.

THE LETTERS

When I first began the Lost Love Project, little did I know how much fun this research would be. I opened each letter and every returned survey with a rush of excitement. The responses impressed me with their readable style and rich content.

Some people requested a questionnaire by scribbling their addresses on dinner napkins, scraps of crumpled paper, or outdated calendar pages. Others sent picture postcards of their cities from around the country and around the world. This was especially true of the Lost and Found Lovers in Honolulu, and they always began their letters with "Aloha, Dr. Kalish." Some postcards came from the hotels where the vacationers were staying when they saw my newspaper advertisement or watched me on television (I received the most postcards from Motel 6).

A noticeably large number of requests came with LOVE stamps. Other people used hearts instead of o's in the words "Lost Love Project" in the address. Some affixed heart stickers, and others painted or drew elaborate and colorful pictures of houses and scenery across the envelopes. Some covered their letters with American flags. The letters from Ireland came with pictures of shamrocks. Some men wrote "Sealed with a Kiss" on the back flap, or put the stamp upside down, a convention that once meant "love."

Inside these envelopes I often found little offerings. Many people sent pictures of themselves with their Lost and Found Lovers, as they had been when they were first dating and as they are now. Some had written poems about their rekindled love experiences, or to their Lost and Found Lovers, which they shared with me. Some wrote essays about their lives in general.

Although I never asked for anything beyond the multiple choice questionnaires, most people included a chronological account of their Lost Love experiences. These stories usually were several pages long. Many rekindled lovers expressed relief and gratitude for the chance to "tell our story," especially those whose relationships ended disastrously, those whose relationships were secret and extramarital, and those whose beloved Lost and Found spouse had died.

Someone who had seen me on *Leeza* six months earlier called the psychology department and told the secretary that she wanted me to find her fifty-one-year-old husband's high school sweetheart so he could "finish some old business." Jody disappointed this woman by telling her that I was not in the business of finding Lost Lovers. (I myself disappointed another two hundred people like that as you will see in Chapter Seven.)

My study of Lost and Found Love was usually upbeat. Reading about beautiful, fulfilling, and healing romances lifted my spirits and gave me a feeling of closeness and kinship with the lovers. I think many of the participants in the Lost Love Project felt the same way. Many of them offered their friendship along with their research contributions. I was fortunate to meet some of these wonderful people during my media appearances and travel, and we stay in touch by phone and letters.

Several couples invited me to their weddings. I attended one reception a few hours' drive from my home: Sharon and Mike were married in Dayton, Nevada, with relatives, new friends, and classmates from their high school class of 1959 to help them celebrate:

MY SOUL MATE AND I went steady during our senior year, thirty-six years ago. We parted because I figured we were too young and needed to meet others before making serious decisions. We each went on to marry others. I divorced, and Mike was widowed.

Mike happened to call a mutual high school friend to see if we were having a reunion. We are a very close class, having reunions whenever one of us feels it's time, every few years. We were never ones to follow the norms. The friend mentioned that I wrote a cookbook and suggested that Mike give me a call. She also called me to say she knew Mike would like to hear from me.

We corresponded briefly, and things took off. We have been rekindling our old flame and getting a lot of airline miles! We find an even stronger attraction and bond with each other than before.

We never really quit thinking about each other, and this reacquaintance was "meant to be."

Some of the respondents had special requests. People who did not want others to know about their rekindled (past or present) romances included complicated instructions on sending them the questionnaire:

⚹ Mark the mail "Confidential" or "Personal." (Some people requested that I put no mention of the Lost Love Project on the envelope, or that I send the questionnaire in a "plain brown envelope." I sent all questionnaires in manila envelopes with the university listed as the return address, not the Lost Love Project post office box.)

⚹ Send the questionnaire only on particular dates (e.g., during a spouse's business trip).

⚹ Send it in care of coworkers, friends, or relatives.

⚹ Send it to a business address, or to a secret post office box.

corresponded with a number of rekindled lovers until they felt assured that their responses were so anonymous that, by the end of the data collection, I might not even be able to pinpoint a questionnaire's country of origin. I did lose a couple of potential participants who feared the loss of confidentiality, including one high-level politician (not from the United States).

Several women wrote to ask me if they should leave their husbands and begin a romance with a recently found Lost Lover. I wrote back that I could not presume to know what is best for someone I have never met, even if I were a licensed therapist, which I am not. One married woman described her relationship with her Lost and Found Lover, and her pain:

THE INSTANT WE SAW EACH other there was a very powerful recognition beyond anything words can describe—like a lightning bolt. I know it makes no sense and there are no scientific cubbyholes in which to put it—believe me, we have tried!

Since that time (two years ago) it has been an intense period.

The relationship has withstood a constant "tug of war" with our moral values. Both of us have a shared faith (thank goodness!), and this is totally out of character for both of us.

We have never consummated our relationship, but that is not to say that there is not intense attraction on both sides. The positive part in all this pain is that my faith is stronger than I ever dreamed it could be, and I am much more able to accept God's will in my life.

It is such a relief to talk about this situation, which must remain so hidden!

The men were similarly torn. True, their preference, unlike the women's, was to begin the affairs and worry about the consequences later, but they did feel the consequences. Several men called in tears, torn between the passion of Lost and Found Love and the stability of spouses and children, homes, and material assets. Almost all of them chose to leave their marriages and start over with their Lost and Found Lovers. These men never expressed any regrets about their decisions to follow their hearts. But their initial losses—of money and property, time with their children, and community status—were considerable, and their decisions to leave their spouses were not made lightly.

THE LOVERS

There is a wide range of individual differences among the participants in the Lost Love Project. For example, they ranged in age from eighteen to eighty-nine—and the eighty-nine-year-old's Lost and Found Lover was ninety-one!

Half of the rekindled romances took place when people were in their late twenties or thirties. Another third were middle aged—in their forties or fifties. Only 7% of the couples who reconnected were in their sixties and seventies, and the percentage dropped to less than one percent by the time people reached their eighties. The story of one couple began in high school, ended, and did not resume for sixty-three years:

HE WAS MY FIRST BOYFRIEND. It was all very innocent. Mostly we were good friends. We walked home from school together, and went out a couple times. My parents didn't like him for some reason. Neither one of us remembers why we broke up.

We went on to long marriages with other people. Sixty-three years passed, and we were both widowed when we went to our high school reunion. I knew as soon as we saw each other. We got to talking and nothing else mattered. It seemed like something that was destined to happen.

We were married on my eightieth birthday. He's so loving and kind and caring and understanding and peaceful. He doesn't argue. He's very respectful, a perfect gentleman. I just love everything about him. He's all I ever wanted.

Two thirds of the Lost Love Project participants were female, and one third were male. But a large number of couples wrote that they filled out the survey jointly, even though the woman listed herself as the respondent. So it is clear that a substantial number of men participated behind the scenes, and my percentages understate male interest and participation. In fact, during the two years that I collected rekindled romance data, almost all of the telephone calls I received were from men, and they were much more emotional about their love— whether joyous or brokenhearted—than the women callers.

I purposely designed the questionnaire with no assumptions about sexual orientation. The survey included two parts to the gender question—one for the gender of the respondent and another for the Lost and Found Lover—and revealed five gay and four lesbian couples. One man in his fifties contributed this story:

IN 1980, I MET MARTY while on a trip to Washington, D.C. At that time I had been with my lover for eleven years and I was unwilling to leave him. So I ended the relationship with Marty.

My lover died years later from AIDS. We had been together for twenty-one years. I had a Names Project Panel made for him and began to contribute to the project as a "Friend of the Quilt." A couple of years ago, I received a copy of the *Friends of the Quilt Report* and saw my Lost Lover's name, also a contributor. Several months later, I came home from work and saw an envelope in my mailbox. I didn't recognize the handwriting. When I looked at the return address and saw that name, my heart skipped a beat. He had seen my name in the same report and had the Names Project forward a letter to me.

It has been almost two years now and we are still together. He now, as before, gives my life passion and I love him *dearly!*

And this story came from a woman in her sixties:

WE MET AT A TEACHERS' training college in Asia when I was in the Peace Corps. She was a teacher there. I served an extra term to be with her. Then I brought her back with me to New York, where she pursued a master's degree in education. My parents liked her and saw our love and affection for each other.

When she finished the degree, she had no choice but to leave the country and go home. This was before the women's rights and gay/lesbian rights movements of the late sixties, and we just didn't know what to do. Obviously, if we had been a straight couple, we could have married and solved the immigration problem that way, but marriage is not an option open to two women.

I stayed behind and became involved in the politics of those civil rights movements, along with the anti–Vietnam War sentiments. I was in two long-term relationships with women during those twenty-five years of our separation. But thoughts of my Lost Lover, and the deep bond of love that we had shared, always shadowed my other relationships.

I went back to visit her in Asia a couple years ago, and we renewed our romance. Again we are stuck with immigration requirements that cannot be met because we cannot marry, so we have lived together six months out of each year since we renewed. We are very happy being together again—a great gift!

The educational level of the participants was varied, but generally high. Only two people reported having a junior high school education. Twelve percent attended high school; 56% attended college; and 32% had gone on to graduate school or professional school after college.

Income levels were also varied but high. Almost half of the participants earned between $20,000 and $59,000 yearly. More than a third of the participants had even higher incomes: $60,000 to "$80,000 or more." Four percent of the sample refused to answer the income question, making it the one left blank most often in the survey. Those who did leave it blank noted that they "do not give their financial information to anyone." (But they did answer the survey questions on sexuality.)

Although the survey asked no questions regarding disability, ethnicity, or religious affiliation, four participants mentioned that they were blind, and some people volunteered that they were Hispanic, African American, Asian, or American Indian. Religions that were volunteered included Catholic, Jewish, Muslim, and Protestant.

I intentionally sampled as wide a variety of regions and cultures as possible to lessen any effects that might be caused by the romantic customs of one particular geographic area. All fifty of the United States, the District of Columbia, and one territory are represented by at least one participant in the Lost Love Project, and there are respondents from thirty-five other countries as well (see Appendix II).

But this wide geographical distribution may not be important. At least five years elapsed between the initial romance and the renewed romance, and many more years might have elapsed since then. This large span of years increases the likelihood that one or both of the Lost and Found Lovers would have relocated. For example, one fifty-five-year-old man wrote:

I'M DANISH. I VISITED ISRAEL in the sixties and stayed with the family of my Lost Lover (she was then fourteen). We didn't become involved until over ten years later, when I again visited Israel. After a month, I returned to Denmark. She married, and made her home in New York for fifteen years. We met again in Denmark.

Married six months later in New York. We're now happily married, with two children, living in Denmark. It's romantic and it's a privilege.

One couple in the survey covered five countries during an extramarital renewed romance over several years, before their respective divorces and subsequent marriage to each other. In another instance, a romance leading to the remarriage of the Lost and Found Lovers took place across continents:

> I MET MY LOST LOVER in Paris in the fifties, and we continued a relationship for three years. I returned to the United States to finish college, and she married an American soldier. I later went to work in the Middle East and Southeast Asia, she divorced, and we married in 1960. I lived with her until 1979 in the United States and Paris. We divorced but kept contact, even though she went to live in Canada. We remarried in 1994.

So my geographical list, compiled from the addresses to which I sent the questionnaires, cannot tell the whole story of each couple.

The Lost Love Project participants are people from all walks of life. They volunteered that they are students or teachers, prisoners, doctors and nurses, lawyers, and homemakers. Some are retirees, and a few wrote from nursing homes. There are published writers (two sent autographed copies of their books), scientists, administrators, computer specialists, and small business owners (who sent discount coupons for their products). Some are cashiers, some sell clothes, or cars, or real estate, and a few drive commercial trucks or buses. At least three are members of the clergy.

They live on farms or ranches, in city high-rise apartments, suburban houses, university dormitories, hospitals, collective settlements, or on-the-go RVs. In short, they are wonderfully average people. You might even know someone who participated in the Lost Love Project.

But do not try to guess whether a story you read in these pages was written by your friend or neighbor (or worse, your spouse). Identifying information has been changed to protect the confidentiality of the writers, and the accounts may have been paraphrased to excerpt long stories into short passages. But none of the stories or people presented in this book is a composite. Each of these stories is a factual account of a real rekindled romance.

After two years of listening—in print, by phone, in person, and by computer—to well over one thousand Lost and Found Lovers from all over the world, I have found the answers to my original questions, and far more. I wrote this book to share this special type of love with you.

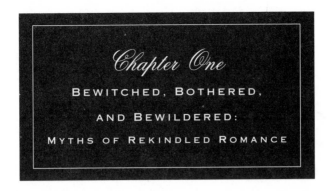

Chapter One

BEWITCHED, BOTHERED,

AND BEWILDERED:

MYTHS OF REKINDLED ROMANCE

I'VE ASKED MYSELF COUNTLESS times why I placed the phone call to my Lost Lover. It wasn't done with the conscious thought that renewing our old love relationship would be the outcome. Maybe it was the idea that I was turning the "Big Five-oh" that made me want to rekindle old friendships. Back then, we were friends long before we were lovers.

We talked that day on the phone for two hours. After that, I found myself thinking about my Lost Lover constantly. One night I got out of bed and wrote down all the events I could remember. Most were humorous, and I found myself laughing out loud as I listed them. I began to think that she would also enjoy reminiscing, so I sent her my list. The response was another list—with additional events I had forgotten!

Now, ten months later, we have seen each other about eight times. Our relationship is *very* intense. It is as if our love was put on "pause" over thirty years ago and then mysteriously once again put back into the "play" mode.

One of the feelings we have is a physical *aching* for each other. We long to talk, kiss, and hold each other, skin to skin. We have sent mushy cards and tape-recorded messages to listen to when we cannot be together. Even if our relationship never results in marriage, our experience over these past months has been a most satisfying one and an experience that can never be taken away from us.

So many things seem to be happening in our relationship for

some spiritual purpose. For instance, I had been out of town on a business trip and had not read a local paper for two weeks—until the day I picked up the paper which had the article about your Lost Love Project. It all seems to be fate.

*T*his story from a middle-aged man in the northeast is one of more than a thousand Lost and Found Love stories returned with the multiple-choice questionnaires. Checking boxes was easy but not satisfying to these lovers. They needed to tell their stories. I could understand that. One of the things that my Lost and Found Lover and I did quite naturally during our reunion was to talk about our initial relationship and our renewed love to anyone who would listen. Our reconnection seemed so rare, so magical, and indeed many people reacted to our story as if it were the perfect fairy tale.

I have learned from my research that this excitement and need to "tell our story" is common. Many people who responded to the Lost Love Project enclosed newspaper articles announcing their weddings, with "then" and "now" pictures. Others added paragraphs or even several pages to the comments section of the questionnaire to fill in the details of their initial love and reunion. Or they sent separate letters detailing their experiences. Most shared the same emotion: "I can't believe this unique and wonderful experience has happened to me!"

But is rekindled romance unique, or even rare? Although it is commonly believed to be, the Lost Love Project revealed uniqueness to be only one of several myths that have grown up around the subject of Lost and Found Love.

MYTH #1: UNIQUE UNION

One man in his fifties, feeling like the Lone Rekindler, wrote to me for help:

THE ARTICLE ON YOUR RECENT study as appeared in *Stars and Stripes* was read to me yesterday from Germany. It was a comfort to us knowing we are not alone in our recent actions or feelings.

Sharon and I were to be married after graduation, but we split just a few weeks before the planned wedding. I went into the service shortly thereafter and we lost touch. Years later, after a brief search, I located her. She is married.

We found in our reunion the long lost love and magic that we once had. Our love is strong and mutual, but we have had many questions as to why this happened at this point in our lives.

We thought we were alone and unique in this rekindled romance. Didn't know who to talk to for guidance. I would like to obtain a copy of your study. We don't know where all this will take us, but any further reference material suggestions you may have or counseling recommendations would be greatly appreciated.

I noticed something else as I told my own Lost and Found Love story: Often my listener would respond by telling another story of rekindled romance. My teaching assistant told me that her grandmother had recently married her high school sweetheart after more than fifty years of being apart. Another teaching assistant volunteered her boyfriend's mother's story. A student had a sister who was married to a Lost and Found Lover. And as I flew on my many trips across the country that summer to be with my Lost and Found Lover, I often had a seatmate, or even a flight attendant, who was in a rekindled romance. I began to question whether this love was really as rare as we lovers assume it is.

Newspaper journalists tend to treat these stories as uncommon. Reporters interview the reunited couple, publish their smiling pictures, and typically write with a tone of fairy tale wonder. Television talk shows use this topic so often that the same host might feature several different aspects of the issue in a single month. One day, happily reunited lovers might appear. Another day is reserved for those who just think about reuniting. Often the host surprises guests by reuniting them on camera with their former sweethearts. Or the topic is reunited first loves, reunited divorced couples, reunited high school sweethearts. The Lost Love theme appears many times each year, yet it is always presented as though it were rare. (Talk shows hardly ever feature Lost and Found Lovers who reconnected but then separated again—usually a devastating experience. The shows are skewed to happy endings.)

In her book about sexual passages, *The Eternal Garden,* author Sally Wendkos Olds found a surprising number of couples over the age of forty who had renewed love with a former sweetheart. She also found, as I have, that this reconnection was almost always a significant turning point for these lovers. Most people in my survey report their Lost and Found Love as a very intense, emotional connection, especially if they had been each other's "first love."

One reason Lost and Found Love appears rare is that it is often purposely kept invisible. In the Lost Love Project, more than 30% of the renewed romances have been secret, extramarital affairs. I have received numerous stories in which the Lost Lovers—happily married to others and up to that point entirely faithful to their spouses—had no idea that when they met for a simple lunch together sparks would rekindle the fire. These couples often asked me to send the questionnaires in care of special confidants.

So my two years of research have led me to believe that rekindled romances are not uncommon, but are simply one of the many ways people find love. When I ask people at random throughout my day, or a large class of students (more than one hundred), if they have ever rekindled a romance themselves or know anyone who has, usually some say yes. My guess from this exercise is that roughly 10% of the population—2.5 million people in the United States alone—have tried to return to a former love.

Finding a Lost Lover is really just an aspect of the more general, and even more common, experience of rediscovering somebody with whom we share emotional past history. For example, I lost track of one of my childhood best friends, Margie, after I moved to California. We reestablished our friendship fifteen years later when I learned that she had breast cancer, and I telephoned her immediately. After that, I wrote letters to her weekly, and she wrote when she felt well enough. We had known each other since second grade, and Marge often filled in little details of my early childhood that I had forgotten. No new friendship, no matter how solid, could give me back those old pieces of myself.

As time went by, we made amends for having hurt each other long ago. Our rediscovered friendship became very important to both of us. We felt as close as if we had never been estranged. All this is very much like what I and so many other Lost and Found Lovers report about our romantic Lost Loves. My correspondence with my dear lost and found friend ended only with her death from breast cancer two years later at the age of forty-four, and she is truly irreplaceable in my life.

Some couples experienced a double reunion: They had lost, and found, a child as well as each other. When the girls became pregnant, sometimes the teen fathers could not face the responsibilities of having a child. In other cases the parents would not allow their children to marry. Some of these young women had abortions, but most gave their babies up for adoption. In later years when these couples reunited and married, they searched for their lost children. Or the women found the children first, then located the Lost Lovers, as was the situation for this woman in her forties:

MY LOST LOVER AND I were forbidden by our parents to see each other after they discovered I was pregnant. With lies they told us, they were able to keep us apart. I was sent to a "home for unwed mothers" until my son was born, at which time he was put up for adoption. My Lost Lover was told that I had an abortion. We totally lost contact for more than twenty-five years, until such time as I was able to reunite with my son. All he knew about his father was that he had been sent to Vietnam, and he wanted very badly to meet him.

At this point, through family, I was able to get my Lost Lover's telephone number, and I contacted him to see if he would be interested in meeting his son. It was then that we discovered the lengths that our parents had gone to, to keep us apart. He had been told I had an abortion, so he never knew he had a child. We spent a lot of time on the phone, as we lived thousands of miles apart. After two months of talking we decided to meet each other again and find out if we could renew our relationship.

We were married eight months later and are very happy to be together and have a chance to know our son. We feel doubly blessed, and are all back together as it should have been years ago. Our parents, who were instrumental in breaking us apart, are now happy to see us finally find happiness.

Others were not successful in their search for the children. These couples, newly reunited but without their children, expressed to me in their letters that they felt guilt and remorse over their initial decision to separate and relinquish the baby for adoption. Their reunions were bittersweet and did not entirely heal the wounds of the past.

Two women kept the children. They rekindled romances in later years when their adult children searched for and found their fathers. One of these women wrote:

> AFTER NOT SEEING MY DAUGHTER'S birth father for twenty years, we saw each other again when she wanted to see her birth father in person. At that point the father was ready to acknowledge her. Our own reunion was passionate, strong, and absolutely primal in that it had to do with the child between us as well as the original feelings.
>
> We won't end up together, both are married to others. But I suspect the feelings will always be there for us. Very odd, but very very deep on both sides.

So when we consider all the aspects of lost and found relationships, including love, we see that such relationships are not rare at all. We regularly bump into or hear news of people from our past and reestablish old bonds. Or sometimes we search for a Lost Lover: "I wonder what happened to . . ."

MYTH #2: LOST LOVER AS ANTIDOTE

Many people believe that Lost Love searches are begun when the searchers are depressed and desperate, lonely, and miserable, perhaps right after divorce. I did not find this to be true for the Lost Love Project participants, or for myself. Quite to the contrary, people contacted Lost Lovers when they felt especially good about themselves, when their self-esteem was high and they felt at peace. One man from Arkansas described this mood:

I AM NOW INVOLVED WITH an old flame of mine. We've been separated for twenty years, since I left my hometown and married someone else. I was divorced when I attended a professional conference in California. Alone, I walked on the beach in the moonlight, feeling a sense of peace. I was inspired, and returned to my hotel room. It was then I wrote a letter to my old flame.

A woman from New York, who had not seen her Lost Lover for thirty-five years, wrote similarly:

IT'S ONLY BEEN SEVEN MONTHS, but everything tells me this is it. I've never been more sure of a relationship than I am of this one because we have the foundation of knowing we are both "good guys" and can build from there. Right prior to this reunion, I never felt more emotionally healthy and strong—if I didn't, I know this never would have gotten off the ground.

This need to feel good makes sense, especially for those who were the "dumpees" years ago. They want to be at their very best when they see the sweethearts who rejected them in the past. One participant described this well:

IT IS A VINDICATION FOR me. I have taken perfect care of myself—I stay in shape—and he was always attracted to beautiful women. He kept kissing my face at the airport, and after twenty years he was saying, "You're beautiful. You look fabulous." His wife never took care of herself, so I was glad to show myself off to say, "Look what you missed! You screwed up and married the wrong woman!"

MYTH #3: SCHOOL REUNION, LOVE REUNION

Whenever I was interviewed by the media, the first question was almost always "So how many of these couples met again at school reunions?" The assumption had already been made that most people reconnect that way. I have heard it stated as a "fact" on talk shows, and I have seen it many times in magazine articles and newspaper stories.

But that is not true, according to the Lost Love Project couples. As you will see, very few began their rekindled romances at school reunions. Many of the Lost Lovers were not even in the same grade in school—the boys were a year or two older than their sweethearts—so they attended different reunions.

MYTH #4: DANGER! SPEEDING!

Imagine a dinner party at which the hostess proudly introduces her Lost and Found Lover to her friends and relatives. These reunited sweethearts are clearly overjoyed to have found each other again, but her guests think the two have lost their minds. They lecture the sweethearts about becoming too close too fast. They warn that this rekindled flame will soon go up in smoke—the lovers can't really know each other after all those years apart. The lovers walk away, hurt and angry. The guests are hurt and angry, too; their kind intentions have not been appreciated. The party is turning into a disaster.

Permit me to step in and mediate between these warring points of view by offering some insights into rekindled romance.

The Lost and Found Lovers see themselves as not only unique but also uniquely blessed. More than two thirds of the respondents feel that the intensity of their love, emotionally and sexually, is unmatched in their entire history of relationships. One woman in her forties wrote:

> THE RENEWAL OF OUR LOVE has been extremely intense and fast moving. He fulfills my need to be seen, recognized, appreciated, heard; to feel, touch, love myself, gives me the freedom to grow and to be sexually satisfied. We have given ourselves completely to each other. We are soul mates.

Another middle-aged woman, who parted from her Lost Lover originally because of parental disapproval and who is now married to him after a twenty-year separation, expressed similar sentiments:

> WE ARE EACH OTHER'S BEST friend—we read each other's mind. When we put our heads together (literally) we both feel a "current" pass between us. It tickles! We've been married for seven years. I'm still his "bride" and people remark now how happy we are. I really don't think I could survive without him. I was married to another for twenty years, he for twenty-six, but it was never like this.

I asked Martin A. Johnson, M.D., a psychiatrist in Sacramento, California, about the intense emotional, sexual, and spiritual qualities reported by Lost and Found Lovers, and he suggested several reasons for the phenomenon. First, he said, consider the *complexity* of these relationships. The partners see themselves as they were, as they are, and possibly even as they will be—all at the same time. Moreover, according to Johnson, this love represents an opportunity for *continuation*—the chance to connect the first half of one's life with the second. The connection offers a rare opportunity to re-do the past. We have few chances to *cope with our regrets* by acting to reverse the damage of our youth. Lost and Found Love can give us the powerful opportunity to do this.

Perhaps the most important force behind the compelling and spiritual nature of renewed romance is the psychoanalytic theory of *repression*. When the sweethearts separated initially, usually at a young age, the traumas of losing that early love and the need to move on to other partners made it necessary for them to suppress their love. These pent-up longings in the unconscious, suggests Johnson, surface during the rekindled romance, and repressed feelings that surface are usually very strong. As repressed feelings become conscious, people feel a tremendous relief from the anxiety of needing to keep them buried.

Lost and Found Love, Johnson adds, also brings up themes of *conquering death.* The love that died is reborn, so in a sense the people are reborn, often during middle age and old age when people are coming to terms with mortality.

In their newfound state of joyousness, couples can feel especially hurt when their love is greeted with cynicism and skepticism. Unfortunately, this is a typical reaction among the people closest to the couple. One man in his forties rekindled a romance with the girl he loved as a preteen. They are now engaged. He described the reactions of others:

SEEMS AS IF EVEN NOW we always have to prove to family that we're okay. We just want them to accept our love and relationship. Our four children from previous marriages don't like our romance. They just kind of put up with it (jealous maybe).

When we see people we haven't seen for a long time, they are amazed, or shocked, or relive their childhoods with us. We make them feel twelve again, but the look of amazement is pretty wild. But to us, it's like, "Isn't that how it's supposed to be?" Isn't that what love is all about? It was nice to see we aren't freaks when I saw your survey. A wedding is planned soon.

Family members commonly express concern that the lovers are moving together too fast, or that they are "living in the past" and will be hurt when present-day reality hits. If a couple's parents disapproved of the romance, some still feel that the relationship is wrong.

Other parents hold on to their old objections to save face or to avoid feeling guilty that they might have influenced their child to make a wrong decision. Still other families continue to harbor a grudge against the lover for "cruelly" leaving their son or daughter years ago, despite their grown child's obvious forgiveness. Sometimes, when the parents are deceased, the siblings take on this parental stance.

In one case, an ex-husband forced the Lost and Found Lovers apart . . . for a while:

MY LOST LOVER AND I decided to move in together and at last begin our lives together. I wish that I could say we lived happily ever after from that point, but my ex-husband saw to it that it didn't last. He filed a lawsuit to gain total custody of our children and he had the money to keep us in court for a long time.

He convinced me that the only way he'd drop the lawsuit would be for me to leave my Lost Lover. I did, but that was the biggest mistake of my life! A year later, however, he provided me with a way out. He'd had a drug problem and wound up in a rehab hospital from an overdose. No judge would give him custody after that.

My friends convinced me to phone my Lost Lover and see if he'd give me another chance. Luckily he's a wonderful guy, and he gave me that chance. I'm happy to say we will soon celebrate fifteen years of marriage. We are best friends as well as husband and wife!

Some Lost Love Project respondents reported that their sons and daughters see the reunion, and the ignited sexual feelings, as uncomfortably "inappropriate for old people." Or the children might be angry because one of their parents was displaced by the Lost and Found interloper, or because they themselves feel displaced. A woman from the Lost Love Project addressed this problem:

I AM STILL NOT ACCEPTED by his family although we have been married about five years now. I think much of the contention comes from jealousy. I am glad we are far away from them. I have been blamed for taking their dad and taking their grandpa away. I think my husband is glad to be away from this too.

One young woman wrote to me because she was about to embark on a rekindled romance. She added this note:

YEARS AGO, MY MOTHER DIVORCED my father after more than twenty-five years of marriage. Then she married her high school sweetheart. I felt angry at her for leaving my dad. And I was sixteen so this was very embarrassing for me, that she was actually dating someone from high school! Now I begin to understand.

Adult children might worry about their inheritance rights, or they might feel protective of a parent who has been alone for awhile. One woman in her late forties wrote:

MY LOST LOVER AND I just spent the last week together, our first meeting in seven years. He listened to my anger and admitted he was chicken shit for running away from me then. We talked the whole thing out; then we could go forward.

So here I am, back in a hot relationship that is so intense I feel drugged. Am I being an idiot? Or is there potential for a wonderful life-long partner here?

My two adult children came for a visit Monday night, and my Lost Lover was willing to face them and answer their concerns. My son is furious with me that I would even talk to him. My daughter said, "Do what you want, but when you get hurt again don't come to me."

As Grace Gabe, M.D., pointed out in her 1993 *Psychology Today* article, "Rekindling Old Flames," the children are trying to come to terms with a love that predates their other parent and may interpret the rekindled relationship as a suggestion that they should never have been born. Gabe explains that this interpretation can pose a threat to their very identities. One young woman commented about her widowed mother's marriage to her high school sweetheart:

I MUST SAY THAT AS a child of one of these people, sometimes it's a little weird looking at the photographs displayed in the house. There are old pictures of them together in high school sweaters, and at the beach when they were in college. Then there are the recent photos of them in their various adventures. It gives one the feeling that they've always been together—as if the lives they lived with my father and my step-siblings' mother never happened. A strange angle!

Friends, too, might be nonsupportive, offering so much unsolicited, intrusive advice that they ruin their friendships. I experienced this firsthand when my own Lost and Found Love involvement caused friction in two of my long-standing friendships. I avoided these people when it became too irritating to hear constant warnings to be careful, go slow, and consult a therapist. In his book *How To Get Your Lover Back,* psychiatrist Blase Harris, M.D., points out that friends who have experienced failed relationships may unconsciously resent the success of the Lost and Found Lovers and want the relationship to fail. He advises reunited lovers to stay away from such people.

Bettie Youngs Bilicki and Masa Goetz, therapists and the authors of *Getting Back Together,* also caution that old friends might feel jealous if the couple devotes more time to their reunion and less time to the friendships.

Is there any truth to the assumption that rekindled relationships are hazardous?

Strangers react positively to the lovers because they see only the beautiful story; they have not watched the long-term ups and downs. But friends and relatives have known this lover over time. Perhaps they have comforted the lover through a long and painful divorce. Or they have seen the lover make mistakes by rushing headlong into a relationship with a near-stranger who turns out to be less than self-advertised. This Lost and Found Love seems to them to be just another ill-advised adventure.

Indeed, renewed romances *do* move fast. As one woman wrote, "He arrived at 10:30 P.M. and never left!" Another woman, now married to her Lost and Found Lover after being apart from him for seven years, told me:

AFTER VISITING ME FOR ONLY two days, he proposed to me. I said yes and we got married two months later. We could not be more happy we found each other again.

And one of the men added:

YES, WE ARE BOTH ROMANTICS and Pollyannas, but we also have our feet planted firmly on the ground. Friends ask us when the big day will be. Some warn us of rushing in too soon. Our usual reply is, "We've a lot to make up for these past thirty-six years, so why wait?" We will probably marry within six months.

Most of the respondents report that this relationship has been the quickest-forming in their entire love history. But this need not be a red flag of warning for these distinctly different romances.

The real danger is that, once the romance begins again, the lovers risk not just another breakup, but rather the end of their most intense love experience . . . for the second time. One man, aged sixty, living in Scotland, offered this insight:

THERE HAS ONLY BEEN ONE true love in my life. Therefore I am unable to make comparison with any other. I have renewed my romance with the same person four times.

My Lost Lover desired conciliation when it was to her advantage. In other words, I was used. The hardest part is letting go. You may be able to walk away from a person, from a marriage, but how does one walk away from a dream? I cannot tell how, finally, I lost the magic, but then I do not know how I found it in the first place.

As if in a wormhole in space, the relationship becomes a time machine into the past. The Lost and Found and Lost Again Lover will grieve not only for the reunion's ending, but also for the first, long-ago ending at the same time.

Yet the overall rekindled stay-together rate in the Lost Love Project is extremely high (72%) and even higher (78%) for the couples who were each other's first loves. These couples say that they share an emotional and sexual satisfaction unequaled by any other relationship before or since. So it would be a shame to pass up this opportunity out of fear. As one middle-aged woman stated:

MY LOST LOVER NEVER MARRIED, saying he had only wanted to marry me. He told me even after I was married that he would wait for me, and he hoped some day we would be together again. Now that we are together again, it seems like no time has passed even though it has been twenty-four years. We both feel as if we had been "biding time" until we reunited. We feel we have a magic between us that we have never shared in any other relationship!

What is the alternative to reaching this highest plane of love, if not to risk an ending? Friends and relatives might be most helpful and appreciated by keeping their concerns quiet as the two reunited lovers do what they must, at the level of speed and intensity that is normal for these courtships. In Chapter Two, we'll explore in more detail the fascinating emotional dynamics that make these relationships so intense.

MYTH #5: SMOKE AND MIRRORS

When I mentioned to an acquaintance who is a marriage counselor that I was conducting a research project on rekindled romances, she reacted swiftly and harshly. She told me, "Couples who do that are asking for trouble. They're just trying to live a fantasy, to re-do the past. The initial problems will always begin all over again. They are just being neurotic, afraid of moving forward and meeting new people." She admitted, however, that none of her clients had ever had this love history (so far as she knew). What should we make of her belief that these couples' love is mere illusion?

It seems reasonable to believe that the lovers' years apart, along with the accumulated baggage of those years, may have made them incompatible. The lovers are no longer idealistic or carefree adolescents: They might own property, have children, manage careers, and be burdened with other adult responsibilities. They may now live hundreds or even thousands of miles apart. And, yes, sometimes there is a current spouse, fiancé(e), or lover or two. One woman discussed these problems:

ALTHOUGH OUR LOVE IS JUST as strong and real for us as adults as it seemed to be when we were teenagers, and although our values, lifestyles, and interests are still very compatible, it became clear that our relationship has no chance to grow and evolve as long as he is married.

So we will have no contact for about a year until he can make a decision about his marriage. If he stays married, we will remain friends without sexual involvement. If he divorces, we will give our romance every chance to work, even though there are major obstacles to resolve—two demanding careers that we aren't eager to abandon, and we live on opposite sides of the country.

On top of all the new challenges, there might still be issues from the past to be resolved. After all, these people did not stay together the first time. As one woman (not a rekindler) warned:

IT WOULD SEEM OBVIOUS THAT whatever broke you apart would do it again; it is best not to carry a torch. Never go backward!

Another message, from a male nonrekindler, read:

THERE IS AN OLD SAYING in the deep South that "one should never walk over old real estate." Applied to relationships, it's hard to rekindle a flame that has expired.

Will the old problems come back to haunt the couple? Are the Lost and Found Lovers so taken with a fantasy image of each other that they sweep all problems that do exist under the rug? The Lost Love Project rekindlers often asked themselves these questions. One man concluded:

WAS IT JUST REMINISCENCE AND nostalgia? Was it, you can't go home again, or was it, never make the same mistake twice? What was different thirty-five years later? We'd both stopped smoking thirty years ago, and we both had gray hair. Nothing else was different. Except of course, we'd learned a great deal about ourselves and about life and could finally see and appreciate what were the solid parts of the romance the first time around. We'd also developed better vision than we had when we were little, even though we both wear glasses now. No, it wasn't just reminiscence and nostalgia.

Risks? Practical difficulties? Sure, there were plenty of those, but there was absolutely no question in either of our hearts or minds about what to do. I divorced my wife, and we married. Old flames do burn the hottest.

Let's compare rekindled love to the more typical beginning of a romance at the age of thirty or older. In the latter case, with luck, a friend or relative has arranged the meeting and can describe the character and circumstances of the prospective date. Or maybe the two meet at work and begin dating (although this has become a minefield with the current climate against sexual harassment). Or they might meet through the shared activities of their children.

In these situations each knows something about the other, but the knowledge is skin deep, so to speak, and in no way touches the core of what it takes to produce a happy, stable couple. As they become more intimate, a pattern often surfaces that would never be evident in the more casual spheres of friendship, work, or parenting.

And all this assumes that the two have honestly presented themselves. Even when we think we know a lot about a prospective partner, new romance can be a risk.

When we meet without any personalized context—at a bar, a singles' dance, or in a quick, flirtatious exchange at the checkout counter of the grocery store—the potential for being hurt is magnified. To protect ourselves, we learn to hold back, or to pretend to be what we are not. The Lost and Found Lovers, to their advantage, may not have this option. As one woman observed:

I THINK A POSSIBLE REASON my Lost Lover and I successfully reunited is because we liked and loved each other before we learned to hide behind masks or build barriers to intimacy. Great closeness was possible because we were more willing and able to be open to an honest exchange of feelings without fear or hesitation.

So actually it is our connections with near-strangers that are often built on fantasy. New lovers frequently generalize from one positive trait (such as being a good parent) to others (such as being a good partner), which may be risky. Further, couples in the early stages of dating may want and need to see their new partner as Mr. or Ms. Right. When they finally see each other as they really are, all too often the honeymoon is over.

Now compare all this to reunited love. Most participants in this survey were adolescents, often first loves, when they first came together. They lived in the same neighborhood, attended the same school, met at church or synagogue, or shared a hobby or club (the school debate team, marching band, 4-H club, sports). I met my own Lost Lover in a college class, so we had something in common on a daily basis.

Back when most people in the Lost Love Project were young, friendships and romances moved at a slower pace than they do for adolescents and adults today. There was plenty of time to know the person as a friend before anything physical entered the picture. For many of the respondents sixty and older, the initial romance was just a friendship with a romantic attraction, since premarital sex was not commonplace.

William K. Rawlins reported in his book *Friendship Matters* that his interviews with senior citizens revealed that their current best friends were people they had met when they were young, even if these friends now lived far away, and even if they rarely, if ever, saw each other. These relationships were more significant than those with newer friends or even relatives. These friendships were considered irreplaceable, and the death of a dear old friend was cause for deep and long grieving. Old friends, William Rawlins wrote, are "narrators and curators" of our past history. Lost and Found Lovers serve these same functions—and more.

Another study by Laurie Shea, Linda Thompson, and Rosemary Blieszner—of elderly adults in a retirement community—confirmed that old friendships are the most cherished and loved, despite intervening years and miles. These friends, the researchers found, are important because they share a history; reminisce; seek advice; reinforce each other's status (old friends compliment each other often, replacing the feedback that retired people used to derive from their careers and civic activities); share very personal information; and care for each other's needs without keeping score.

Some women who wrote to me, seniors now, added that they were forbidden to go out alone with their young teenage boyfriends. Yet these first romances lasted a surprisingly long time, often three years or longer, compared to the short romances of today's adolescents. One woman in her seventies described her initial romance:

I WAS TWELVE AND LOST Lover was fourteen. We shared a "first kiss." He was afraid of my parents, who were very strict. I couldn't date until I was sixteen, and he left for the War before I turned sixteen. We were neighbors.

I had a crush on him all my life, even after fifty years. We're very compatible, and having a common background takes up a lot of the slack in the years in between.

But we have a lot of differences, too. I'm still working in a good career and he's been retired for ten years. I'm hyperactive and he's laid back. But we're very happy and in love—and like each other as well. I expect we'll get married when I retire next year.

Few adolescents in earlier times owned their own cars, and some in the Lost Love Project had been too young to drive, so parents drove the couples to and from a movie, an ice cream parlor, or a diner. Most still lived at home, so these teens spent time at each other's houses. Many respondents said that the Lost Lover had been regarded almost as a family member. They knew each other's parents and siblings, and watched each other interact in the home environment. All these factors left little room for fantasy and illusion in the initial relationship.

Such background commonalities actually shape couples' attitudes toward loving. A recent study of twins, conducted by Niels G. Waller and Phillip R. Shaver, strongly indicated that attitudes and preferences about love styles, as well as the choice of partners, are due almost exclusively to the environment—being exposed to the same past history of parents, neighborhood, schools, peer group, etc. These early environmental influences on love relationships, Waller and Shaver found, had a lasting effect, even on people who were ninety years old. No wonder rekindled early loves are so compelling and successful!

Although preferences about love do not seem to change over time, people's goals and needs change under some circumstances. This sometimes works to the advantage of the renewed relationship. For example, respondents who wrote about health challenges or about facing death believe they became more loving and appreciative of pleasure afterward.

One woman in her fifties expressed how her drive for achievement affected her initial, Lost Love marriage:

ONE OF MY INSIGHTS IS that I left him because he enjoyed life, because he did not take things seriously. At eighteen, I was driven and took everything seriously. In school and in work I met people who were intense intellectuals, and I did not appreciate his way of being. He surprised everyone a few years later by graduating from college and progressing from teacher to superintendent of a school district. By the time we renewed our relationship, he had taken early retirement and was once again carefree. I had made "my mark," getting most of the intellectual stuff (and being serious for most of this time) out of my system. I was just beginning to embrace life, to laugh at myself and others.

All of the reasons I had been attracted to him at age fifteen, but rejected him at age nineteen, were still there. This time, however, I have a deep appreciation and respect for his values. He brings me joy and he makes me have fun! Were my instincts more valid at fifteen than my intellect, such as it was, at nineteen?

People who abused alcohol or other drugs during the first romance might have changed dramatically by becoming clean and sober. Recovery programs or individual counseling might have helped them counter ingrained destructive habits and values. One man shared his story about the effect of drugs on his Lost Love:

OVER THE YEARS WHILE WE were growing up, we spent many long hours on the telephone, but always as friends. She regarded me as a sort of "big brother type" because I was two years older. When my Lost Lover entered high school, she was constantly pressured to experiment with drugs and alcohol. She would always call me for encouragement and strength, and thankfully I was able to steer her clear of most of the dangerous situations.

About three months after I graduated, I left to go into the service, and she was left pretty much on her own. I would call and write, but I could detect a rapid decline in her personality and values. One day, when I could not get in touch with her, I called her friend and found out she had been placed in a court-ordered drug rehab program in another city and none of her old friends could contact her.

Well, I pretty much gave up ever seeing her again, as I was being transferred overseas. But fifteen years later, out of the blue, she called me at home, saying she saw a letter I had written to the local newspaper. I was no longer married. We talked for over four hours on the phone that night, catching up.

The next night she came over to my house, and the rest, as they say, is history. We are in a loving, caring, adult relationship, something apparently we were not prepared for while growing up. Old friends do make good lovers!

Some women in the survey had launched into long-term therapy for sexual abuse and wrote about the positive results in their lives and particularly in their rekindled romances.

Of course, normal development allows people to become better at solving problems and communicating, and their moral character matures. These changes smooth the way for love the second time around. One man in his fifties reflected upon his maturation and changes for the better:

I EVEN KNEW I WAS wrong at the time, but I couldn't admit it then. I was a stubborn teenager. The years have confirmed that I blew a good thing with unfounded jealousy due to my own insecurities. Since we broke up back then, I've never experienced the same passion or feelings that I had with my Lost Lover.

I've learned a lot in the meantime. It could have been a good match had I matured faster, mellowed, or "cooled" it—but that's water under the bridge.

Not all changes are positive, unfortunately. A large number of survey participants encountered the upheaval of the sixties, with its availability of drugs, *after* the first romance, so it is not surprising that some participants reported that the lover became a drug user over the years apart, with a devastating effect on the rekindled romance. One man admitted to this problem in himself:

MY ATTEMPTS TO MAKE THE renewed relationship work were overshadowed by my insecurity and remaining feelings of rejection. This left me very unsure of where I stood with her and led me to do and say very irrational things. All of this was exacerbated by my burying myself in alcohol and dope. Now that I've cleaned myself up, I really think I can approach another relationship between us a little more rationally.

A woman from Indiana also wrote about drug problems in the sixties:

ON THIS VALENTINE'S DAY, WE saw an article about your research that said you were still looking for rekindled lovers. Here we are!

Dennis and I found each other again after thirty years apart. Our reunion was so moving that we feel God directed us to each other just at this time in our lives. We were married exactly a year after we remet.

We had been high school sweethearts, but we led completely different lives in different parts of the country after we graduated. Dennis joined a band and went to San Francisco in the late sixties, and became part of the hippie movement, complete with the drug experimentation and free love lifestyle. I went to college and married. Dennis also married, then divorced.

During his single years, he did some soul searching and worked on ridding himself of some bad habits. He became deeply involved with Narcotics Anonymous, doing a lot of service work. He's been clean and sober since then.

Meanwhile I raised my family and tried my best to be a supportive wife. But after the kids were grown, I was left staring at a long, lonely life with someone I no longer loved. Then when I saw Dennis again, I had an immediate passionate response. I felt like a kid again, and after a few months of talking on the phone, I realized I wanted to give our love a chance.

I left my marriage and began to see Dennis. After just two weeks I knew I wanted to be together forever. We are the loves of each other's lives and know that God brought us back together to share our mature years. We are the Baby Boomers that everyone talks about. We look forward to retirement, but we feel like teenagers.

Some of the Baby Boomers, as this middle-aged woman expressed, were changed by Vietnam:

WE LOST EACH OTHER OVER his being called up for Nam. I could not support his going. He was into the "John Wayne syndrome" and went on to become decorated and end up in a psych ward upon his return. I broke our engagement. He went through "Jack Daniel crazies." But always, out of nowhere, he'd find me and turn up.

He almost died once and when he revived, he rethought a lot, and that prompted him to call me. After sixteen years, we renewed our wonderful love as though it had never stopped. We lived together, although he was still legally married. And one day I found a new love letter from a liaison he had in Paris, on the same day he professed his undying love, bond, and commitment to me. I don't know if this is all a manifestation of the sociopathic side of his post-stress syndrome, but *I* am the one in therapy, to explore the feeling of the rug being pulled out from under me.

If one or both of the Lost and Found Lovers had been involved in a long and bitter marriage, dysfunctional patterns of relating might have become habitual. The partners may have resorted to belittling each other, yelling, or withdrawing emotionally. Despite the lovers' attempt to nurture the new Lost and Found romance, the behavior patterns of the intervening years might snuff out a rekindled flame.

On the other hand, one woman found that the dysfunction of prior marriages had helped, in an odd way, her rekindled romance:

> MY LOST LOVER, NOW MY husband, and I were both in very dysfunctional marriages for years—horrible! But we get along great and are very happily married. By torturing our former spouses, we learned what *not* to do, and how to treat each other, to make *this* marriage work!

Three women reported that their renewed relationships failed because their Lost and Found Lovers came out of the closet and admitted that they had realized they were gay only after the initial teenage romance years before.

Another major change occured if one of the partners had a mental illness that became more symptomatic with time, as is common with schizophrenia or bipolar affective disorder (formerly called manic depression). Years ago the lover might have had barely noticeable, excusable, symptoms or even none at all. One man wrote of his experience:

> AFTER WE STARTED THE RELATIONSHIP again in our forties, I had the feeling that the trauma she went through in her family years ago had left scars on her that prevented emotional intimacy, but she would not discuss this with me. As an adult, she was also prone to loud temper tantrums.
>
> The relationship ended when I had a relationship with a woman who had a normal range of emotions. This reminded me that no previous girlfriend had ever been so volatile toward me. My Lost and Found Lover was perfectly prepared to forgive my affair, but I chose not to renew this romance.

Most of the people I surveyed, however, saw their partner as essentially unchanged, for better or worse. Each still saw the same youthful sweetheart with the same personality characteristics, the same mannerisms, the same background and family of origin, and the same shared experiences, interests, and values of the original friendship and romance. This is not fantasy, not wishful thinking. It is real.

And this is the point that several of the lovers urged me to stress: Lost and Found Love works because the couple begins by already knowing each other. One man, now married to his high school sweetheart after a fifty-year separation, stressed how important it was to him that he did not have to devote a long time to sharing his background and history, or to learning hers:

> THIS INFORMATION WAS ALREADY, ACCURATELY, in place, which I see as an advantage, particularly for couples in their senior years who feel the pressure of time. The word I feel most characterizes these relationships is "comfortable."

Even the oldest respondents in the study reported that, to them, the lover looked physically the same as years ago. He saw the same teenage girl, and she saw the same teenage boy. They see themselves as suddenly younger, too, which is invigorating and part of the great joy of these romances. One seventy-year-old woman wrote:

> THIS REKINDLED ROMANCE HAS GIVEN us a chance at happiness again. I never forgot him—or never stopped loving him, actually, though I have been married and widowed twice. I feel seventeen again and he calls himself a "seventy-year-old teenager!"

If this is smoke and mirrors, it certainly does not hurt romance!

One woman who participated in the survey summed up the general feelings quite nicely when she wrote:

> BECAUSE WE GREW UP TOGETHER and I knew his family, I feel I know him and can trust him in a way I've not previously experienced.

A man in his early sixties, who rekindled a romance after more than thirty years, only to have it end again, provided these insights:

> WHAT HAVE I LEARNED? OH, my . . .
>
> 1. True love, I mean gooey, kissy-face, rip-snorting LOVE of the romantic type poets sang and wrote about long ago does exist! I was convinced that it was fiction until three years ago.
>
> 2. We make decisions which affect our whole lives when we are just teenagers, with no experience, no frame of reference, and sometimes with no luck. It's as if you have only one chance in a contest, and you don't know the rules, and your life depends on it.
>
> 3. Love gives meaning to life. Love means that when you die, somebody misses you and regrets your passing. So while you live, show some class, be nice to people, leave the world a better place.

4. People rarely change in a real sense. A person who is a weakling as a child will probably be a weak adult, psychologically. Character flaws are timeless and permanent, as are strengths.

5. It's better to know than to wonder. If the answers are available, go find out and put your mind at rest.

I am grateful for the catharsis afforded by the writing of these thoughts to someone who might appreciate the musings of a sixty-one-year-old ex-doctor who finally got some answers to the queries of a lifetime. We finally had the honeymoon we missed so many years ago. I will love her forever. I am thankful that I finally got the ragged ends of my life tied up at last. Too soon ve grow oldt. Too late ve grow schmart, ja? Auf Wiedersehen.

These romances are not only real and comfortable, then, but also among the best relationships ever encountered by those in the Lost Love Project.

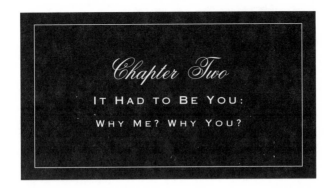

Chapter Two

IT HAD TO BE YOU:

WHY ME? WHY YOU?

ANY REKINDLERS IN THE LOST Love Project were not content to check boxes on a questionnaire or write their story. They wanted to talk. They telephoned to ask me: Why was this unexpected love happening to them? Why was it happening with someone from long ago? Why now? Why was the love so passionate and overpowering? How would they choose between a faithful family and a retro romance soul mate? Would the love last? If not, how could they handle a second ending?

What are the characteristics of rekindled romances and the Lost and Found Lovers who pursue them? After several years of research, I can provide some answers.

WHY BOTHER?

Bookstores are filled with self-help books that describe how to find the perfect lover, how to stop making mistakes in love, or how to heal a broken heart and learn to love again. A viable alternative to this serial monogamy is to reignite an old flame, but few books present this as an option. One book that does is *How to Get Your Lover Back,* by psychiatrist Blase Harris. Dr. Harris offers insights about renewed love, and about the longing for it. In particular, he describes the need "to discover that your lover is coming back, sooner or later is coming back, that you will have another chance." What makes this hope so persistent is that, as Harris says, "relationships rarely ever really die, with the kind of finality that physical death has, so long as both partners are still alive." One woman confided in her letter to me:

> OUR RELATIONSHIP IS SUCH THAT it is always as if time had stood still. Even from our first reunion, we could not believe it had been almost fourteen years since we had met. It was a very brief relationship then, and yet very powerful. This relationship is the major topic of my therapy work at this time. I feel we should be together, that it is right and everything else is wrong. We are compatible in so many ways—soul mates—and even when we attempt to end the romance we move toward each other after a period of time.
>
> I wish he would seek counseling, too, so he could move forward with me or end it. All I know is that I am happiest when I am with him, feel most fulfilled, loved, and cherished than I have with any man before.

Why do some people continue to think about an old flame, while others seem to move on? And why do we think about a *particular* old flame? Psychologists James E. Collins II and Leslie F. Clark conducted a series of experiments that indicate that people whose relationships were ended by their Lost Lovers experienced more stress, depression, and obsessive thoughts about their former lovers if they perceived themselves as having made a large investment (of time, effort, money, or compromise) in that particular romance; lacked a clear understanding of what happened to cause the breakup; and thought more about the details of how they fell in love than about the details of the ending. These people also rated their Lost Loves as being "less over with" than did people who understood their past romances. My research bears this out: A noticeably large number of Lost Love Project participants indicated on their questionnaires that they had had many lingering questions and loose ends about this *particular* early romance before they renewed it and talked about it with the Lost and Found Lover.

WHO BOTHERS?

Some people might think about their Lost Lovers or even contemplate searching for them, but for some reason they do not. One man wrote to tell me he contemplated a rekindled romance but soon changed his mind:

> AFTER MY DIVORCE, AND AFTER learning that my childhood sweetheart was also divorced, I made a half-hearted effort to relocate her after a vision in an airport.
>
> But then I decided something was wrong with that vision, for by now she was twenty-five years older, and has had experiences far different from mine. Author Thomas Wolfe was right, you can't go home again. I moved on, found another, and am now satisfied that I made the right choice, that I did not disturb another life in the name of "nostalgia."

Not all visions and dreams caution against rekindling a romance, of course. I have found that many of the respondents of the Lost Love Project are deeply spiritual or religious, and are truly convinced that their Lost and Found Love was made in heaven. For example, one woman wrote:

> WE THINK IT IS A miracle, our individual hearts' desires were heard and answered and we were reunited at a wonderful event—a "house blessing." My roommate invited my Lost Lover (unbeknownst to her or to me, of course) when she met him at church and thought he was a very nice man (understatement).
>
> When he arrived and announced his name, that was when the magic happened. I told everyone, "This is my first love from college . . . how did you get here?!" and the whole room came unglued, everyone was squealing and laughing.
>
> We've been talking, laughing, crying, hugging, and enjoying life together ever since. This loving relationship is effortless, full of growth

and risks. I love this man. He is my brother, best friend, lover, nurse, and partner in living a more and more conscious life each day. Thanks angels, (Oneness), and God.

In a different spiritual vein, one man wrote:

> I WAS PLAYING THE Ouija board with some friends. I asked the supposed spirit, "Who am I going to end up married to?" Those *exact* words—and the board wrote out my then-ex-girlfriend's name. I thought it was impossible, but after marrying and divorcing someone else, I guess the Ouija board was right!

Dr. Grace Gabe described some other characteristics of rekindlers in her *Psychology Today* article. She found that people who try a rekindled romance tend to be optimistic and action-oriented throughout their lives. She notes that they are risk takers; they are not afraid of love as an adventure. One widowed woman in the Lost Love Project confirmed this:

> THE MOMENT I SAW MY Lost Lover (after forty-five years apart), those feelings of long ago returned with such great intensity it frightened me. It was just unbelievable. For me, there is no question that I would like to spend the rest of my life with him. The chemistry between us, as well as the nostalgia, is just incredible. I am definitely a risk taker and a romantic person. The changes in our appearance and years apart have not diminished the emotional connection. This has all been such a wonderful fairy tale.

Rekindlers often manifest romantic and poetic traits, as in this example submitted to the Lost Love Project by a fifty-year-old woman:

> MY LOST LOVER AND I met when we were four years old at our small town's playground. We went to school together (K–2). In kindergarten, my love stole a ring from his mother's jewelry box, and

we became "engaged." My family moved to the city, but we continued to see each other all through elementary and high school (he hitchhiked on the weekends, or when school was out because of deep snow), and I was his date for the junior and senior proms. We were best friends.

I went off to work in an office and he went away to college, so we took separate paths. Years later, however, I was in my home town on business for a week, so I wrote my Lost Lover a letter at his mother's old address. He called me and the rest is history. We have been married for six years and have a deep and passionate relationship!

Another woman wrote of her romantic reconnection after more than thirty years:

WE WERE TWO FIFTY-YEAR-OLDS ACTING like love starved sixteen-year-olds. We felt so young and alive, we laughed until our sides hurt. We cried together and we prayed together.

Our first meeting was like a fairy tale romance. When I arrived in California from New Mexico, my Lost Lover was standing at the gate with a dozen roses, he had a musician singing love songs, a limo was waiting for us, and all of his friends who did not even know me.

We danced together right there in the airport and thirty some years melted away. The whole rest of our time together radiated with love. Strangers commented to us on our love. We are waiting to marry each other, as soon as geographic locations (our occupations and families) are resolved.

The Lost Love Project did not inventory personalities, but the comments and stories I received were worded so identically that it seemed as if people all around the world had rehearsed with each other what they would say:

- This is the person I should have married.
- During our time apart, I always loved my Lost Lover.
- I looked for him/her earlier, but I couldn't find him/her.
- We were meant to be together. We are soul mates.
- If we can't trust this relationship, we can't trust anything.
- God brought us back together. We have a spiritual connection.
- We regret that we didn't have children together.
- No one ever knew me or understood me as completely as my Lost Lover.
- Every day with my Lost Lover is precious. I don't want to miss even one.
- I know now what I lost, and I could never leave my Lost Lover again!

And if I may offer an educated guess about Lost and Found Lovers: Those who have loved and lost, but who are willing to trust and try again, must have a strong capacity for forgiveness.

WHEN TO BOTHER

As Dr. Harris writes in *How to Get Your Lover Back,* the timing of the reconnection is important for success. Although the focus of Harris's book is not necessarily on long lost lovers, but rather on those who might have separated just weeks or months before, he offers valuable information for any couple considering a reunion. He warns that reunions should be avoided until the former lovers can let go of their neediness and anger. In addition, if one of the lovers forces the romance back together, resentment instead of renewed love will result.

In *Getting Back Together,* Bettie Youngs Bilicki and Masa Goetz emphasize that the couples must stay apart long enough to rest and recuperate; to face the causes of the breakup and find workable solutions; to end knee-jerk reactions caused by painful memories and by dysfunctional ways of interacting; and for each partner to build a separate, independent life and make essential changes within himself or herself.

In the Lost Love Project, a minimum of five years intervened between the initial loss and the reunited romance. These years gave the lovers an opportunity for growth and a fresh beginning. Romances renewed after five to ten years were common but did not last as long as those that were rekindled after a longer separation. So the fairy tale Lost and Found Lovers who were parted for thirty, forty, or fifty years might actually have had an advantage over those seemingly easier renewals after a mere five years or so.

WHEN NOT TO BOTHER

Not all relationships should be rekindled, of course. Some marriages and romances *should* end, because they are destructive. There are "impaired lovers," says Harris, who are abusive, dishonest, and manipulative. Impaired lovers criticize and pick fights. Their goal is not to love, but rather to win, to be in control. Getting back together with an impaired lover who has not changed is asking for trouble. One woman in her fifties offered her unfortunate experience:

> I COULDN'T BELIEVE THAT AFTER so many years of being divorced, I married my Lost Lover, a man whose profession (bus driver) kept him constantly away from home. And my children did not like this man! I discovered after we married that he was emotionally and physically abusive. He claimed that his marriage before me had failed because he longed for me. How silly I was to believe that. And while on the road traveling, he was seeing other women (they even had the nerve to call our home sometimes).
>
> I asked him to move out and I got a divorce. Our relationship started as a love story and ended as a horror story. He took quite a bit of money, too. I ended up burning everything I had saved in memory of him—all the letters, pictures, everything. I felt so stupid to have kept all those things for so many years. I look back now with regret and anger instead of the nice memories I once had.

Other impaired lovers appreciate only the initial, romantic stage of falling in love. Their relationships might be long but typically will be disappointing. Or they might choose serial monogamy: constantly new, temporarily perfect lovers who provide idealized highs. This emotional pattern can be seductive and can continue for years. It might account for the try, try again couples in the Lost Love Project. Each reunion has more intensity and puts more at stake for the couple. One middle-aged woman wrote:

> I TRIED TO BE VERY clear to him this time not to make this another drop-in of once every four or five years. I wanted this to be *It*. But he has not called after his first month of renewed contact. I have taped music for him to listen to. I composed a journal to pour out my grief, feelings, questions. I will always love him, no matter what becomes of our latest reunion.
>
> He said he wanted to spend the rest of his years with me. He told me that I am "for real," not wanting him for anything but him— not for his money, possessions, etc. It all sounded so real to me when he said it. His family is thrilled that we are back together because he is soooo happy. But they do not know all the facts, and I will keep it that way.
>
> I believe we are soul mates for life and beyond, and all of our other couplings in our respective lives mere fill-ins for what once was between us. I still measure all men in my life by him. I wish apathy were possible with him, but the spirit remains no matter how many sage sticks, musk incense, incantations, books, and tapes I use to try to exorcise him out of my space. Keep in touch to find out how my soap opera turns out.

Rekindled romances are dangerous for people who are obsessive, because if the romance ends again and the Lost Lover cannot let go, it may require years of counseling to heal the damage. One Lost Love Project respondent in his thirties wrote:

> THIS WAS PROBABLY THE MOST traumatic experience I ever had. For me it didn't work. She was engaged to someone else at the time and got me to think that she was prepared to leave him. I

became physically and mentally ill, and if this study can help someone else, then I have made my contribution.

Probably because of shock I became frozen and experienced physical discomfort in my shoulder and neck. I've been on antidepressants since we split up.

A letter from a young woman told a similar tale of obsession and despair:

MY PARENTS DISAPPROVED OF MY Lost Lover, but we continued to sneak to see each other for the next four years. But I broke it off abruptly after meeting a man whom my parents greatly liked. With this news, my Lost Lover tried suicide.

Time passed and I needed to find some peace, so I called him. Over the next few months we had many telephone conversations, and I fell in love all over again. We agreed to meet but he never showed up.

In the past couple years, my pain over him has brought me to near-suicide at times. Sometimes I have been an obsessive lover—calling him, writing him letters and poems, sending him gifts. I know I would give up almost anything in my life to be with my first, lost love. Hopefully this story is to be continued.

Some love mistakes are caused by misinterpreted feelings. The classic research study by D. Dutton and A. Aron in the *Journal of Personality and Social Psychology* (1974) showed that anxiety can be misinterpreted as sexual arousal if the anxiety takes place in someone's company. This and further studies explain why an office romance might begin (under pressure from a work deadline, perhaps). It can explain why people who experience anxiety caused by jealousy conclude that they must be truly in love, why passionate sex might accompany a secret affair or follow an argument or abuse, and why Lost and Found Lovers keep trying to reunite over and over when it does not lead to happiness. This information might help one woman in her forties who wrote about her secret Lost and Found romance:

OVER A YEAR AGO, I contacted this guy that I could never get out of my head. We had dated only briefly, yet there was something so primal about our roots that I just never forgot him.

Since that phone call after a twenty-year hiatus, we have been in regular contact. While this romance has given me a tremendous emotional satisfaction, I am disturbed by the fact that there has also been so much pain. For example, while I have never been a jealous person, it bothers me that I feel this way when my Lost Lover tells me about the women in his past and present life. He is single; I am not. Before I married, I used to date a lot, but I never felt one twinge of jealousy with anyone before, not even with my husband.

I am still searching for an explanation for why I feel as strongly as I do towards this guy. I apologize for the anonymity; however I must preserve my identity. Most people would be shocked if they knew about this other life that has been so important to me. Thanks for investigating this subject!

People who offer dysfunctional repetition, obsession, idealization, and anxiety are not really loving. It is best to leave those Lost Lovers lost.

WORTH THE BOTHER

Erich Fromm defined love as "the active concern for the life and growth of that which we love." Using that definition, Harris likens real love to possessing a magical recording of music "that changed a little each time you played it, sometimes going back to the original but varying endlessly in pleasant ways. You would never tire of it." This is what renewed love offers at its best—the original, changed a little, varying endlessly. One woman in the Lost Love Project gave this account of her husband's generous love and commitment:

WE MET IN HIGH SCHOOL when I was fifteen and he was sixteen. Instantly, and I mean instantly, there was a bond between us that was wonderful, however terrifying to me. This young man was completely in love with me and told my mother he would marry me someday. He was one of the social outcasts because he was so advanced mentally, so he was the school nerd. I didn't want to feel the way I did about him since dating him made me unpopular, and at that age fitting in is so important. I kept going off to relationships elsewhere, then going back to him after every attempt failed.

We did marry. We were happy until he was laid off at his job. I began to think that being married wasn't fun, so I told him that I wanted a divorce. As always, he only wanted my happiness, so he gave me the divorce even though it almost killed him.

I remarried and had a son, but I realized after seven years that contrary to my foolish belief, not every man would love me like my Lost Lover did. He stayed in touch with my family, and through them he knew the difficulties I was going through. We reunited after I got a divorce from my husband.

After almost eleven years to the day from our first wedding date, we remarried. Being married to my Lost Lover is even more wonderful than I ever imagined it could be. Because we share so much of a past, we are closer than ever.

We celebrated our first anniversary last month, and this was very special because we were only married nine months the first time. We sipped a toast to the years ahead and to the years behind, no longer disillusioned by youthful, unrealistic ideals but clearly understanding how precious true love really is and cherishing the love that endured all the pain in between.

When I talk about rekindled romances, most people smile, then tell me about their own memories of "a very special person" from years before. Sometimes, as the smiles fade, regrets set in. They confess to lacking closure—explanations or apologies that were never given, dreams that were cut short, questions that still linger. Contact with a Lost Lover can put the past to rest, and even redefine the last years of one's life. Not all of the Lost Lovers remained together, but still, most rekindlers in the Lost Love Project felt that the reconnection had been worthwhile.

OST AND FOUND LOVE has been part of human imagination and fascination for centuries. It is part of our cultural heritage and permeates the media. Renewed love has mass sales appeal: The J. Peterman clothing catalogue, known for its romantic stories that tell a tale about the clothes, recently included a story entitled "Thirty Years Later," about a chance romantic reconnection "on a steamer off the coast of Norway." And Marriott Hotels mailed out an advertising brochure picturing a thirtysomething couple lying on a lawn, smiling serenely, her head and arms draped over his chest; the copy reads, "Room 920. Want to remember why they were high school sweethearts." The inside of the brochure continues, "It may not be easy to reconnect these days, but we believe: when you're comfortable you can do anything."

Lost and Found Love plays a role in the mystique that surrounds certain celebrities. To the best of my knowledge, none of the respondents in the Lost Love Project is a nationally known celebrity, although some have achieved prominence in their careers. Their love experiences, however, are no different from those of the rich and famous: "It's still the same old story," as the song from *Casablanca* tells us. Because we know the experiences can happen to anyone, we follow celebrities with a special fascination.

The pattern of love/separation/reunion is so pervasive in our culture that sometimes we do not consciously notice it. But we know we feel cheated if the lovers remain apart. *We are socialized to expect rekindled romance.* Let's look at some examples of real and fictitious rekindled romances that have quietly but persistently influenced our ideas about love.

FAMOUS REMATCHES

Novelists and composers often borrow from their life experiences to create fictitious characters and situations that sometimes involve Lost and Found Love. In the mid-1800s, composer Giuseppe Verdi renewed several romances. According to *Verdi: A Biography,* by Mary Jane Phillips-Matz, his first Lost and Found Lover was soprano Giuseppina Strepponi. After numerous separations and reunions in cities across Europe, the two began to live together openly and later married. Interspersed with his relationship with Strepponi (sometimes even in her presence at the same hotel) was his passionate love for another of his lead opera singers, Teresa Stolz, again with separations, and lasting until his death at age eighty-seven. As if that were not enough, his letters over the years referred to his on-and-off love for an unspecified woman he called "the Angel whom you know." It is no wonder, then, that his operas (such as *La Traviata* and *Aida*) reflect sorrowful separations and tragic reunions.

A composer of another sort, just as famous in his own time, Jerry Garcia, may have broken his high school sweetheart's heart twice. A recent press release about the estate of the Grateful Dead musician stated that Barbara Meier filed a creditor's claim alleging that she and the rock guru were Lost and Found Lovers, and that he had promised to marry her in 1992. He backed out, but agreed to pay her $3,000 every month for three years. In 1994, he married another woman. According to the press release, Barbara Meier says that he paid almost all of the money promised, but that his estate owes her $21,000 because payments were cut off by Garcia's wife shortly before he died.

Most of those who participated in the Lost Love Project were sweethearts in high school, or even earlier, during the initial romance. More often than not, the romance was with their first love. Similarly, the actors Melanie Griffith and Don Johnson were teen sweethearts who married in 1976 and divorced a year later, partly because of their youth and partly because of the dysfunctional patterns that often accompany alcohol abuse. They remarried in 1989, with maturity and abstinence in their favor, and even costarred in a movie with a rekindled love theme, *Paradise*. Even after Griffith filed for a second divorce after Johnson's relapse with alcohol, she continued to refer to him as her "soul mate." I think we have not heard the last of this couple.

Compare this with the rekindled love experience of Elizabeth Taylor and Richard Burton. Their initial romance, along with their marriage, also took place during a period of substance abuse (alcohol and prescription drugs). As was probably the case with Griffith and Johnson, the extreme behavior that so highly correlates with substance abuse caused their separation and divorce. But the Taylor and Burton reconnection did not take place in an atmosphere of abstinence. Nothing had changed when they married for the second time, and the rematch was doomed just like the initial experience. Many couples in the Lost Love Project had this marriage/divorce/rematch pattern, sometimes successful, sometimes not.

Will Fowler and Hal Jacques published an article in *Remember* magazine about a rekindled romance between two celebrities who married and divorced. She married someone else, but after that marriage failed five years later, the original couple renewed their Lost Love. She rejected his many pleas to remarry, although he was always there when she called to say she needed him, and she remained very close to him until her death at the age of only thirty-six. Her Lost and Found Lover took care of the funeral arrangements and delivered red roses to her grave once a week for the next twenty-five years. He never remarried. That Lost and Found couple was Marilyn Monroe and Joe DiMaggio.

Strong emotions are part of the fabric of rekindled romance. The tragic death of DiMaggio's Lost and Found Lover released his deep and long-lasting sorrow. And reconciliation attempts can ignite turbulent rage. For example, one man wrote from prison to share his story:

MY FIANCÉE AND I WERE girlfriend and boyfriend thirty years ago. Fate set us in different directions. We got back together recently, and plan to marry soon. The emotional love and sex, mentioned in the newspaper article about your project, is something we thought no one else would understand.

Everything is very intense, even fights, thus my current residence. We argued one night and I slapped her. She called 911. I get out in a few months. What I did was wrong, I know that. I have hurt her before, always when we both drink. But I was married before for thirteen years and never touched my ex-wife, sober or intoxicated.

Do you have a guess as to why I would hurt Kathy? Is it due to the extreme, elevated feelings? She still waits for me, but I don't want to come back here again, and I am afraid to return to her. And her jealousy is almost a crime. She says, "Mess around and I'll make Lorena Bobbitt look *mild.*"

I think you need to look at the bad side of these very emotional relationships!

NFL Hall of Famer and actor O. J. Simpson stood accused of killing his estranged wife and her friend. At the time of Nicole Simpson's violent death in 1994, the Simpsons were divorced and a reconciliation had just failed. It was revealed during his trial that O. J. had erupted in raging arguments with Nicole. The failure of his rekindled romance could have sent his anger over the edge into a double murder. But the jury disagreed with the prosecution and he was acquitted.

For many couples in the Lost Love Project, the rekindled romance began as an extramarital affair. Some eventually married, after divorce or the death of their spouses. The late statesman W. Averell Harriman and his wife Pamela followed this pattern. As discussed in Christopher Ogden's biography of Pamela Digby Churchill Hayward Harriman, *The Life of the Party,* the two met at a dinner party during World War II, when Pamela was twenty-one years old and the then-married Harriman was forty-nine. Their affair lasted two years, until Harriman went to Moscow. But his financial support lasted much longer—until their respective spouses were deceased and they were free to marry each other, almost thirty years later, in 1971.

Woody Allen renewed a relationship with a Lost Lover in the form of a friendship. After his romance with Diane Keaton ended, a mutual respect remained. She was his leading lady in several films, including *Annie Hall,* a semiautobiographical account of their romance (Keaton's real name is Hall). Since the ending of Allen's "marriage" to Mia Farrow, Keaton has again appeared in his films.

Similarly, some participants in the Lost Love Project built platonic friendships the second time around, sometimes because they did not want to jeopardize a marriage, sometimes out of fear of another breakup. One woman even named her son after her Lost Lover (with her husband's knowledge and consent) though she had not seen him in many years. Later these two Lost Lovers renewed their ties as platonic friends, because they are both married to others.

In the late 1980s, Garrison Keillor married a woman he had not seen since high school. She had been an exchange student from Denmark. The American press hounded him and treated the romance as an eccentric whim, until he felt compelled to move with his wife to Copenhagen to escape the publicity. The marriage ultimately fell apart, perhaps in part due to these external strains.

The Lost Love Project includes several people who fell in love when they were foreign exchange students. The reason that their initial romances failed was not just the geographical distance after the exchange student went home. As in Keillor's case, the romance was not taken seriously: The Lost Lovers' parents belittled this love. A woman in Oregon—once an American exchange student in Germany—expressed this:

I CAME BACK TO FINISH high school in the United States. In the time we were separated, we both dated other people. We reunited last summer in Germany. We plan to marry after we both finish our graduate programs.

He is coming over next Christmas to meet my parents for the first time, although they do *not* like him. They have a hard time accepting the *idea* of him. They are afraid I will move to Germany and they'll never see me again. However, they are slowly accepting it.

I believe they thought the first time we were together was a "brief fling abroad," but now they realize it is much more serious.

Sometimes love cannot bloom the first time because of the extreme age difference between the two lovers. President Grover Cleveland married a woman he had known much earlier as a friend of the family. His wife, Frances, was twenty-one and he was forty-nine at the time they married, but he had been a close friend of her father since she was very little, when he had bought her toys and dolls. After her father's death when she was only eleven, she became even closer to Cleveland, and their contacts remained frequent through her high school years, dimming when she went away to college. It was during these years that he began to have romantic feelings for her. When she graduated, Cleveland proposed to her by letter, and Frances accepted. A Lost Love Project respondent also remembers her current husband from when she was very young:

I AM NOW FORTY-FIVE. WHEN I was very young, maybe five, I was very fond of a young man who was the grandson of the woman who lived next door. He was in college when I was in kindergarten. In later years he married, and I was the baby-sitter for him and his wife. I was always fond of him, always happy to see him.

Years and years passed, until I was four years divorced with small children of my own. I heard from a relative that he was also divorced. At the moment I read that sentence buried in the middle of a chatty family letter I felt my heart leap out of my chest. It was like that scene in *Alien* when the monster bursts through the guy's sternum at the dinner table. I heard myself say out loud, "This is the man I'm going to marry." I knew this was completely crazy. We were on opposite sides of the country, I hadn't seen or even heard from him for years, and I could not have told you what he looked like or what kind of work he did. I tried hard to ignore this feeling for a few weeks, gave in, and wrote a brief sorry-about-your-divorce note so I could get on with my life.

Of course—you guessed it—he wrote back, a long letter, and we began a wonderful correspondence, tentative at first, then more and more intimate as time passed. He said he had always thought I was special, and thought of me from time to time; as a college man, he wondered why he would think of this childhood girl, but there it is. When my love, after six months of letters and then phone calls, walked off the plane to be with me for the first time, he was fifty-two and I was thirty-seven. First time either of us ever went to bed *before* a first date. It was, and still is, fabulous, every time.

We have been married now for eight years, and every day is a gift, a delight, a wonder. We have hard times sometimes, but nothing will ever separate us.

In President Theodore Roosevelt's case, both were too young the first time around. His second wife, Edith, had been his neighbor when he was a young child; she was his sister's playmate. After the death of his first wife, he ran into Edith by chance at a gathering held at his sister's home. They began to date and eventually married. One couple wrote with a story like Roosevelt's:

WALTER AND I WERE BEST friends when we were four years old, and neighbors, forty years ago. Our moms were also friends. We enclose a photo taken when we were about five; it was taken in Chicago one hot summer day as we shared a Popsicle. (We recently used this "Popsicle picture" on our wedding invitations.)

I would always go to visit Walter to play. Only if he was busy would I go play with my girlfriends.

When Walter was eight he asked me, then six, to marry him someday. After he promised that we could live on a farm and have horses and cows, I said yes.

But my family moved away, and I lost touch with him until high school. My family went back to Chicago to visit. I was so excited to go see Walter, but he was with his buddies. He came out of a back room and just said, "Bye, I'm leaving." It broke my heart.

Our moms stayed in touch, so I knew when he married, and he saw my wedding pictures. We both figured that that was the end of any relationship between us.

But two years ago I went to visit Walter's mom when I was on a business trip nearby. We had a great time chatting about old times. After I left, she called Walter and said, "You really should see Susan!" It had been more than thirty years since we last saw each other. We met for lunch the next day, and we felt as if no time at all had passed. We could talk about anything so comfortably, and we laughed about childhood memories.

We had both divorced by then, so we exchanged telephone numbers and addresses. Over that next year our feelings renewed, and we fell in love as adults. We have just married, forty years after Walter asked me the first time. He has ten acres with cows, and plans to get horses for me—to fulfill his childhood promise.

Much has been written about President Franklin Roosevelt's affair with Lucy Mercer, Eleanor's social secretary, in 1914 and 1915. When Eleanor learned of their relationship, she threatened to divorce Franklin unless he stopped seeing Lucy. He agreed. But they rekindled the romance a number of years later, and it is generally believed that Lucy was at Roosevelt's deathbed in 1945—and was whisked out before Eleanor arrived.

No doubt there are many other high-profile people with Lost and Found Love histories. One couple's reunion may even affect a country's future government. Prince Charles and a woman he loved before his marriage, Lady Camilla Parker Bowles, have been the subject of much speculation in the press over the years. His Royal Highness has now publicly acknowledged that they have rekindled their romance. They fell in love when he was twenty-three, and they were together from 1972 until she married her Lost and Found Lover in 1973, while the prince was away in the Navy. They rekindled their romance in the late 1970s, and his correspondence indicates that the new romance continued until his engagement to Lady Diana, in 1981. Then another rekindled romance between Prince Charles and Lady Camilla began in 1986 or 1987, according to the prince, hastening or directly causing his separation from Diana.

Prince Charles's admission that Lady Camilla has been his one and only true love, her divorce, and his recent insistence on being seen with her in social circles prompted Queen Elizabeth, and some government officials and British citizens, to call for Charles to divorce Diana. Although he has now done so, some people still believe he should give up his claim to the throne. In fact, the continuation of the monarchy itself is in some doubt. The crown could bypass Charles and pass to his son, but press accounts have suggested that the British public may lose patience with the royals altogether and abolish the monarchy.

That seems like a lot of damage from one Lost and Found Love that just won't quit. But I believe that those who have experienced their own surprisingly powerful renewed romances can understand the importance and intensity of this romance for Prince Charles and his Lost and Found Lover. The Princess of Wales deserves equal compassion for her love and marriage, burned and destroyed by a rekindled match.

EPIC REUNIONS

I have received many telephone calls and letters from people asking me to recommend some books that feature the rekindled romance theme. There is certainly no shortage of such literature. The theme of lovers who separate and then reunite is one of the oldest in print. We have been taught from our early reading experiences to expect renewed love, even when the sweethearts in the book seem hopelessly separated. Our own romances must be influenced by all of this cultural conditioning.

But are these accounts accurate? How do Lost and Found Lovers in print compare to actual rekindlers? Let's take a look.

The first account might be found in the Judaic version of Genesis (Bereshith)

25:1: "And Abraham again took a wife." The Hebrew word for "again" is interpreted by early Jewish sages to intimate that Abraham remarried his previous wife, i.e., Hagar. (Six percent of the Lost Love Project couples had been married and divorced years ago.)

During the Middle Ages, the love songs and poems of the troubadours celebrated the spiritual ideals of courtly love: The knight chose a noble lady to worship; he would then go off on a quest and perform brave deeds on her behalf. This love was not to be physically consummated, nor did it lead to marriage. Indeed, the beloved lady was usually married to someone else. The precise form that courtly love demanded was codified into thirty-one rules during the reign of Queen Eleanor of Aquitaine, and written down by Andreas Capellanus between 1182 and 1186. Among them were the following:

* Marriage is no real excuse for not loving.
* He who is not jealous cannot love.
* The easy attainment of love makes it of little value; difficulty of attainment makes it prized.
* When a lover suddenly catches sight of his beloved, his heart palpitates.
* He whom the thought of love vexes eats and sleeps very little.
* A true lover is constantly and without intermission possessed by the thought of his beloved.
* Every lover regularly turns pale in the presence of his beloved.

I incorporated some of these ancient rules directly into the Lost Love Project questionnaire. Many people indicated by their answers that these courtly ideals continue to be relevant in modern times.

In the early medieval poem cycle of Tristan and Iseult, Tristan sets off to perform noble deeds, and to carry Iseult the Fair back for marriage to his uncle, King Mark. But Tristan and Iseult fall madly in love with each other after they mistakenly drink a magic potion meant for King Mark and Iseult, and they act on their physical passions. Although Iseult marries King Mark, the potion has bound her to Tristan, and the two meet secretly.

As was the case with a few of the Lost Love Project couples, King Mark discovers his wife's unfaithfulness and forces the lovers to separate. Before they do, she gives Tristan a jasper ring and promises to return to him if ever a messenger comes to her bearing the ring. In several Lost Love Project stories, a ring figures prominently, as in this account:

> MY LOST LOVER SAYS HE'S been in love with me for forty-five
> years! He never forgot me and on our first date when we got back
> together he gave me his high school class ring again—the one I sent
> back to him over forty years ago when I broke up with him. And as
> he gave me the ring he said, "Every time I looked at it, I thought of
> you, and it belongs with you." I now wear it on a long gold chain
> every day. We plan to marry next year.

This token of love proves to be the downfall of Tristan. He eventually marries another woman, but on their wedding night the jasper ring falls off his hand and clatters onto the stone floor. This reminds him of his devotion to Iseult the Fair, and he is then unable to touch his wife. When she learns why he has never consummated their marriage, she becomes bitter.

Finally, as Lord Tristan is dying, he sends for Queen Iseult, and she sets sail immediately upon seeing the ring. But his vengeful wife lies to him, telling him that the ship flies a black flag to indicate that Iseult the Fair is not on board. Tristan dies of grief before Iseult reaches the shore. When she arrives she realizes what has occurred, lies down at his side, and dies from her own sadness.

Some respondents in the Lost Love Project reported that their spouses angrily destroyed tokens from the initial or rekindled stages of the Lost Love relationship. Many others wrote that they hid the Lost Lover's photographs, letters, or gifts from jealous spouses, sometimes even when there had been no contact between the two Lost Lovers for many years. In one case, a woman hid old photographs of her Lost Lover for forty-eight years, until after her husband's death. Two years later, the Lost Lover, himself widowed, coincidentally telephoned her, and the two reunited and married.

In death, Tristan and Iseult are reunited. King Mark buries the lovers on opposite sides of a wall. But one night a strong-limbed briar bush springs from Tristan's tomb, quickly climbs the wall, and roots at Iseult's tomb, where it remains for many generations, bearing beautiful blossoms.

The theme of a reunion after death appeared in the Lost Love Project letters and comments as well. Some people wrote that they believe they will never again be separated from their soul mate; even after they both die, they will be together in spirit, literally or figuratively. In one touching questionnaire from a widower:

I MET MY LOST LOVER when she was ten years old and I was eleven. We dated all through high school, then we were separated during my tour of duty in Vietnam. At that point she soon broke off the correspondence and hastily married someone else. I married also, but we both eventually divorced our spouses, reunited, and married each other. Sadly, she was diagnosed with an incurable illness six years later, and died several years ago.

In answer to the question "At This Point, If You Are Separated from Your Lost Lover, Does It Feel as if Your Relationship Is Permanently Over?" he checked "No."

Another respondent firmly felt that her deceased Lost and Found Lover was still in her presence. Throughout the questionnaire, she checked the box for "We Are Still Together" along with the box for "He Is Deceased." She did not want me to think that this was a mistake, so she wrote:

THOUGH THE LOVE OF MY life, my Lost Lover and my husband for wondrously happy years, is now deceased, I still feel his presence and his love all around me. I think that we shall never be separated, ever again. This is not a morbid worship of the dead, but a joyful appreciation of the fact that we had a loving, soul-joined marriage and a thirty-year friendship that has made every facet of my life precious.

In his book *We*, Robert A. Johnson proposes that Iseult the Fair represents the Jungian concept of *anima*, i.e., the ideal (and therefore unreal and unattainable) woman, the "feminine" side of the soul. If a man is not willing to acknowledge those aspects of himself, the ideal becomes projected onto a real woman, and only disappointment and suffering can ensue when her fully human weaknesses become evident. One man wrote to me, portraying how his Lost and Found Lover helped him discover hidden facets in his own nature and rekindle with his wife—an interesting and happy ending, compared to Tristan's fate:

MY FIRST LOVE REMARRIED. NOT long afterwards, my daughter began college in the small town in Massachusetts where my Lost Lover lives with her husband. My wife and I went there for a Parents' Weekend and had lunch at their house.

And do I still love my Lost Lover? You bet I do, and everyone knows it. And I always will, but we are both happy in our separate lives. It was so important to me to tell her after thirty-five years that I still loved her. It helped heal old wounds that I had buried deep inside me.

She came into my life as "a wakeup call," and my wife and I heeded it. She sent me a copy of Robert Johnson's book *We* and it gave me the insight that I needed to repair my marriage.

Her husband is a wonderful man, but she was afraid to make a commitment. I helped her say "yes" and now she is blissfully happy. And so am I.

Now my life is at a higher level. I understand poetry and Shakespeare as never before. My wife and I are coming up on our thirty-fifth wedding anniversary, and we have more passion than ever. Every day we look for ways to keep our love and marriage strong.

I am very happy that you're doing this study. First love is a powerful emotion.

Lost and Found Love has many characteristics of the passionate courtly love romances. The initial phase, when most of the lovers were quite young, and especially if they were first loves, is a stage of idealizing the sweetheart. The lovers have few or no other love relationships to compare to the Lost Lover, so that person will not fall as short of expectations as later lovers might. In addition, adolescence tends to be a developmental period during which friends and sweethearts are idealized.

After this spiritual idealization comes the later separation of the couple, and perhaps hardships and disappointments are encountered during their time apart. Like the lady and her knight who returns from the quest after all the dragons are slain, the reunited modern lovers are dearer to each other because of the time lost and the hardships endured. One woman, who married her Lost and Found Lover after they had been apart for twenty-six years, commented on this:

> SOMETIMES I REGRET MISSING SO much time with him, but I have five beautiful children to show for those years. And if I had to live through all of the pain and abuse to get where I am today and to appreciate what a beautiful person he is, then I guess it was worth it.
>
> I have to be one of the luckiest and happiest people in the world. Every morning I wake up, look at Ray, and thank God for letting me find him again.

Despite the lovers' idealization of each other, rekindled love is rooted in reality because of the couple's shared initial history and comfortable feeling and their new maturity. It is the rare combination of these two elements—the romantic and passionate courtly love idealization along with the ordinary love born of human relatedness—that makes these Lost and Found Lovers so compelling and their love so lasting.

FAIRY TALES OLD AND NEW

In the Tristan cycle, men were expected to perform brave deeds to prove their worthiness. Other forms of old stories, such as fairy tales, often emphasize the psychological lessons that are learned during the lovers' separation. According to the late psychoanalyst Bruno Bettelheim, although a myth is grandiose, described as miraculous, and usually ends tragically, a fairy tale is told as if the characters could be anybody ordinary; the events are described as ordinary (no matter how unrealistic); and the story usually ends happily. Many Lost Love Project respondents called their rekindled romances "a fairy tale." One couple even married in Cinderella's Castle in Disneyland.

A fairy tale in which the lovers separate and reunite is "Rapunzel," by the Brothers Grimm. The prince, who has secretly visited Rapunzel, is discovered and pushed from the tower by the witch who imprisons her; he is blinded by thorns as he falls. The prince then wanders about the forest eating nuts and berries, lamenting and weeping over his Lost Love. The Brothers Grimm tell us that "he roams in misery for some years" until finally he stumbles upon a desert where Rapunzel has been living in anguish with their twin children (the story never tells how these children came to exist). Her tears of relief and joy, when she recognizes him by his voice, fall into the prince's eyes and cure his blindness. Then they journey to his kingdom for the happily-ever-after ending.

The past suffering of Rapunzel and her prince, represented by the tears, allows him to see his lover clearly (the return of the prince's vision). In like manner, respondents in the Lost Love Project reported that they "now see" how much their rediscovered sweethearts mean to them, lamenting the years apart that "we should have had together." One woman in her forties wrote of her magic kiss of clarity with her Lost and Found Lover:

THE MOMENT I SAW HIM at the airport, all of the other people there disappeared—he was the only one I saw. I walked into his arms and got the most wonderful bear hug I ever had. Then a kiss. It was magic. It was like going home.

The second time we met was again magical, also calmer, richer, fuller. I felt centered. It's as if my feelings for this man were merely suspended in time—just waiting below the surface for that one hug, that magic kiss, to rekindle the love and caring and passion brighter and stronger than ever.

One man in the Lost Love Project wrote his whole Lost Love story in the form of a classic fairy tale, only a small portion of which is offered here:

ONCE UPON A TIME, MANY years ago (even before television was invented), there lived a beautiful princess in the Great Pine Barrens. The princess—who was as pretty as a picture—fell in love with a tall prince who was a pretty good basketball player. The tall prince also fell in love with the pretty princess, and they were very happy together.

Although the prince loved the princess very much, he did not really know how to love (he was young and immature). But he knew he would soon go away to college, so he just pretended that he didn't love the princess anymore. He ignored her and dated ladies-in-waiting. The princess dated others, too, but neither the tall prince nor the pretty princess was happy.

Now it just so happens that every four years, back in the Great Pine Barrens, the Pom Pom Queen summons all of the subjects back for a "reunion"—an opportunity to get together and look at pictures of their children, grandchildren, and even great-grandchildren, and to see how much older and maybe wiser everyone has become.

So the tall prince went to the Ramada Inn where the now-grown-up princess was staying, to meet her and take her to the banquet. The minute he saw her, the tall prince was not nervous anymore. He felt comfortable, and by the end of the weekend, the tall prince had fallen in love with the now-grown-up princess all over again. . . . All the subjects were very happy about this, because this was the way things were forty-six years ago, so it made *all* of them feel much younger. And the pretty and now-grown-up princess and the tall prince lived happily ever after. Of course!

As in courtly love romances, the time that two fairy tale lovers spend apart, and especially the suffering each endures alone, contributes to their personal growth and appreciation of each other when they finally meet again. It deepens their love. As Bettelheim writes in his book *The Uses of Enchantment,* "The rescuers fall in love with these heroines because of their beauty. . . . Being in love, the rescuers have to become active and prove they are worthy. . . . The stories seem to imply that falling in love is something that happens; being in love demands much more." It is no wonder, if Bettelheim's analysis is accurate, that rekindled love is even stronger and wiser than the initial romance.

While the Brothers Grimm were writing their fairy tales, the novel began to come into its own as an important literary form. Lost and Found Love appears often as a major theme. A few classic examples include Jane Austen's *Persuasion* (a friend takes a parental role to force the lovers apart); Charlotte Brontë's *Jane Eyre* (the lover is already married); James Whitcomb Riley's book in verse *The Girl I Loved* (the girl thinks her suitor is too poor); and F. Scott Fitzgerald's *The Great Gatsby* (the woman is indecisive).

A more recent novel (1988) is *Love in the Time of Cholera* by Nobel Prize winner Gabriel García Márquez. The story centers on a woman named Fermina Daza, who has married a wealthy doctor, and Florentino Ariza, the man she had promised to marry when she was a schoolgirl, who has never married and loves her still.

He is what one would have to call a patient man. He accepts her life with her husband. He simply waits until the day the man dies before offering his love again. Like Ariza, several men in the Lost Love Project admitted that they read the daily obituary notices in their Lost Lovers' hometown newspaper, "just in case." One man, now in his fifties, wrote:

SHE FINALLY TOLD ME WE are through. I think not. I'll outlive her husband if she doesn't leave him first. I shall prevail one way or another: second-generation German stubbornness. The only thing I want to do in this life before I leave it is to make her happy in my company.

Despite hundreds of sexual liaisons which are of no consequence to him, Florentino has waited for his Lost Lover for more than fifty years (he knows the exact number of days they were apart). He ultimately persuades Fermina, with his letters, to rekindle their romance. Again, like Ariza, a Lost Love Project respondent from England also courted his sweetheart with correspondence:

MY LOST LOVER WAS MY first true love. She was sixteen and I was eighteen. The year was 1942. Our love was very deep and intense, but parental discouragement ended our relationship. Memories of our courtship were never erased, nor did they fade with the passage of time. We later discovered that our dreams and fantasies about each other over all those years were uncannily similar, deeply emotional, and deeply erotic!

After we parted, I moved away. I made some visits back over the years, always hoping, anticipating, that I might meet her again by pure chance, but it never happened. One day, however, a compulsive need and desire to trace her overcame me. My enquiries were successful and we arranged a short meeting. I will never forget seeing her seated at a little table in a tearoom waiting for me. She was even more beautiful than I remembered, so elegant, serene, her hair still the color of golden corn. I instantly fell in love with her all over again.

Subsequently we met at infrequent intervals for the next few years, over intimate lunches, afternoon teas, sightseeing car rides, and each time feeling more intensely connected. Finally I had the courage to tell her my feelings. From that day onward we corresponded frequently, our letters becoming increasingly emotional, and on my next visit a year later, culminated in our becoming true lovers. One might say that I seduced the beautiful lady with my letters!

To enjoy such a beautiful and fulfilling love fills us with such gratitude and happiness, our personal miracle. She is the perfect lover of my dreams and fantasies, and she says I am hers, too. Daily I give thanks for being blessed with such love. I quote to her over and over a line from a letter written by a French artist: "Ton amour est pour moi—ma Vie" (Thy love is for me—my Life). I feel that says it all!

When the relationship of Fermina and Florentino finally becomes sexual after all those years, it is one of the rare descriptions in literature of the physical love of a couple in their eighties, with all their joy, as well as their embarrassment and insecurity about aging bodies that could only appear beautiful to Lost and Found Lovers. As García Márquez writes, "They were satisfied with the simple joy of being together."

Some of the most recent novels about Lost and Found Love include Anita Shreve's *Where or When* (so immediate it reads just like many of the letters I received); David Lodge's *Therapy* (a lighter search for a childhood love); and surprisingly few romance novels.

Yes, I probably overlooked some readers' favorites. But an exhaustive coverage of all of the books featuring Lost and Found Love would have me still writing into my golden years. So I have selected works representing a variety of times and places, yet incorporating the same issues and situations faced by the current Lost Love Project respondents. Besides, these are *my* favorites!

REKINDLED FLAMES ON THE STAGE

One can always find Lost and Found Lovers in an opera house. Grand opera is grand passion, and what could generate more feelings of physical longing, jealousy, anger, despair, exhilaration, bliss, hopefulness, and hopelessness all at once than a rekindled romance?

Inevitably, two lovers in opera separate, and often reunite only as the heroine is dying (*"addio,"* she sings). The amount of time they are separated might actually be very brief, but the audience would never guess that from watching the lovers' intense grieving in the parting scene and during their separation, along with the frantic passion of their reunion. If these were actual contemporary lovers, their friends would surely recommend counseling or a self-help book on love as an addiction.

For example, in Giacomo Puccini's *La Bohème,* Mimì and Rodolfo separate, and it is only a matter of weeks later that the Lost and Found Lovers reunite, just before Mimì dies of consumption (tuberculosis). *La Bohème* also contains a subplot of rekindled romance: Musetta and Marcello argue and separate and reunite repeatedly. The tragic love story of Mimì and Rodolfo is echoed in a story told by a woman in the Lost Love Project:

TEN YEARS AGO, I WAS living in California at the end of a crumbling marriage, and becoming totally stressed out and ill. I moved back to my hometown for medical treatment. I had never forgotten my "true love" (really my only love), whom I met during World War II. Our situation was hopeless and we parted and married others. Through my unhappy years I continued to think about him. Back in my hometown, I searched and found him. He, too, was divorced after many unhappy years.

It was wonderful to become reacquainted. We had fun times together, enjoying so many of the same things. He was a diabetic and had already had a massive stroke and a heart attack. But he seemed very well under the circumstances. After we had spent almost three years together, he complained of feeling ill, so I took him to the hospital. They said he was all right, so I took him home. However, he died very suddenly.

I like to think he survived through major health problems so that we could share some quality time together. I will never forget him.

Another woman wrote about her brief but spiritual reunion:

I FELL IN LOVE WHEN I was nineteen and my Lost Lover was twenty-two. But he had already promised to marry another woman, and he kept his promise.

I saw him occasionally until about twenty years ago. Then we lost contact. For the last year, I had a strange urge to find him—a need, you might say. When I did, I also found that he was dying.

A very wonderful thing happened between our two families. My Lost Lover said God had sent me, and our families seemed to believe it, too. I spent every minute I could with him. He died in my arms two months later.

His wife and children thanked me for loving him and making his ending easier. My husband had only asked of me that I save a place in my heart for him. It was as if they knew that it was meant to be and just backed away and let us be in love for sixty-three magical days. It has changed my life.

Another popular opera by Puccini ends on an even more tragic note. In *Madame Butterfly,* a Japanese woman named Cio-Cio-San (Madame Butterfly) waits for "one fine day" when her Lost Lover, U.S. Navy Lieutenant Pinkerton (in fact, he is her husband, wedded in a Japanese ceremony which he never condescended to regard seriously), will return to her. Although she has actually been abandoned by Pinkerton and does have another suitor, she loves him and regards herself as married.

When he returns to Japan, he brings his "real" American wife with him. He is there to take the son he fathered with Cio-Cio-San back with him to the United States, which he considers to have a superior culture. When she hears the cannon fired by his approaching ship, she awaits him, dressed again in her wedding dress, but her hopes for a rekindled love are dashed. Instead, Cio-Cio-San is to be left alone, without husband or son, in shame and unbearable grief. Instead, she chooses death with honor, and the opera ends with her suicide. One woman in England wrote of a Lost Love experience similar to the Butterfly story, albeit with a less bloody ending:

WHEN I WAS SEVENTEEN, I met a boy of twenty-two, my first love. Against my parents' wishes we got engaged, but after a few months we argued and parted and he went into the Army.

Years passed, and I wanted to make up with him. I tried to trace him through his family and through Army personnel. This went on until I was in my late twenties and I did trace him.

He finished in the army, came home, and we got together again. I went to live at his family home and we got engaged again. Shortly after the engagement, I got pregnant so we planned to marry sooner than anticipated. However, when I was approximately three months pregnant, his wife and child showed up!

His family and I were devastated! Apparently he had married whilst abroad in the army and told no one. I subsequently left his family home but couldn't return to my home because of the stigma attached to the situation in those days.

Fortunately a lovely lady I had only met once took me in. I had the baby, a girl, but had to have her adopted, again because of my home situation. Happily now I am reunited with my daughter through her efforts to trace me.

If the Lost and Found Lovers do not share the same feelings and expectations, or if one of them is unavailable, the stage is set for despair. One Lost Love Project participant wrote that her sanity was at risk, that she was "on the edge," after the breakup. A few participants expressed gratitude to Prozac for lifting their depression. A man developed panic attacks. And two women acknowledged that they attempted suicide after their Lost and Found Lovers left them.

When Richard Wagner fashioned the opera *Tristan und Isolde,* he changed some details of the poem cycle, but kept the Lost and Found Love element. Opera critics have often focused on the brooding tone of the music. Wagner's own life no doubt contributed to the despair and sense of hopelessness that permeate the opera: He was deeply in love with the poet Mathilde Wesendonck, his friend's wife. Their affair further damaged Wagner's already miserable marriage, and it is believed that he modeled his ill-fated Isolde and Tristan after Mathilde and himself.

Another Lost and Found Love story of the stage is about the phantom who lived in the Paris Opéra. *Phantom of the Opera* entertains audiences nightly, from

Broadway to California. Christine and Raoul had been childhood friends. They parted ways, then saw each other briefly as adolescents; it was just enough time for Raoul to give Christine a kiss on her hand and tell her, his first love, "I will never forget you."

Years later, when he attends the Opéra on a night that Christine is singing, they catch a glimpse of each other. She writes him a letter "as the little girl that I then was." We can hear in her statement echoes of the Lost Love Project respondents who felt young again after being in contact with their Lost Lovers. Raoul responds with a visit and they rekindle their adolescent romance, despite the "phantom's" jealous rage and the deadly obstacles he uses to impede them. But their Lost and Found Love is so strong that even the phantom cannot deny them happiness together.

Kern and Hammerstein's *Show Boat,* first performed on Broadway in 1927, is based on a book by Edna Ferber. It includes a story line about the lost and found romance of eighteen-year-old Magnolia, the boat captain's daughter, and a river gambler, Gaylord Ravenal. The curtain descends with the couple's reunion—and his reunion with their grown daughter—twenty-three years after their separation.

A musical from the 1950s, *Fanny,* also reunites the child with the father, as well as reuniting the Lost Lovers. In this play, Fanny, a teenage French girl, falls in love with a young sailor, Marius, who leaves port despite fathering a son. To erase the stigma of bearing a child out of wedlock, Fanny marries Panisse, a wealthy older suitor who wants an heir and rears the child as his own. Fanny and Marius are able to renew their love years later, with the blessing of Panisse as he is dying. The family is united at last—just like the Lost Love Project couples who had a child during their first romance and reunited, together with the child, years later.

In *Carousel,* the reunion occurs after Billy Bigelow's death. Billy returns from heaven to visit his fifteen-year-old daughter, whom he has never met, and Julie Jordan, his former wife. The meeting with each woman lasts just a few minutes, but it is healing for all of them. Billy regretted that he had never told Julie that he loved her before he died; now he does, and though she does not see him, she "hears" him, and her face lights up into a smile.

Even though some of the Lost Love Project reunions were also brief, they helped people to heal, to put aside hurtful memories from the initial broken romance, or to complete the love bond that was meant to be. One woman had a particularly poignant Lost and Found Love story:

I MARRIED MY HIGH SCHOOL sweetheart after a separation of over fifty years. He had proposed to me when he was eighteen, but he was shy and just said, "What do you think about us getting married?" I didn't understand that he was proposing. I just didn't know what to think, so I didn't say a word. He didn't know what else to say, so he just dropped it at that.

He moved away, and I married. After a time I was divorced, and I stayed single for the next thirty years. One day I saw a picture of his stepmother in the local newspaper. I called her to see what had happened to my Lost Lover. She told me he was a widower. I got his phone number and gave him a call.

He was delighted to hear from me after all the years, and we made plans to get together. He flew back to our hometown, and after a few visits, we knew we had fallen in love all over again. This time when he asked me to marry him, he was very direct! And I said yes.

We were married in our hometown in South Carolina after over fifty years of separation. Our families were very happy for us. They knew what we meant to each other, and could see how happy we'd become in the recent months we spent together. But our bliss was tragically interrupted by his death just a few hours after the wedding. He was buried in his wedding tuxedo.

I enclose some newspaper clippings of our love story. After you read them you may come to the same conclusion that I, our friends, and family have come to. We find comfort in knowing that his dream was fulfilled: that he returned to his hometown and married his first love, and that he was happy when he died.

And I would rather have had those few months with him than a lifetime with anyone else. Those wonderful memories will last me all the rest of my life. I feel complete.

As a last example of rekindled romance on the stage, what could be more appropriate than the longest running play in the United States? Jones and Schmidt's *The Fantasticks* opened in 1960 at the Sullivan Street Playhouse off-Broadway. Although most new musical plays in New York and London are very expensive productions with elaborate sets and special effects, it is interesting that the longest running play takes place on a simple stage consisting of a platform and four poles, with a cast of nine actors, a cardboard moon, and a handful of glitter.

The plot is simple, too. Hoping for an adolescent rebellion, two fathers pretend to feud so that Matt will fall in love with The Girl Next Door, Luisa. The charade works, but they are starry-eyed teenagers, in love with love as much as with each other. The romanticism soon wears thin, and they yearn to leave home and experience life. And so they do, with all the disappointments, mistakes, surprises, and suffering that accompany humans as we mature. When Matt and Luisa finally rediscover each other back home, they realize how much their young love has meant to them. One Lost Love Project respondent stated this as a theme in her life:

> WE REALIZE NOW THAT WHAT the two of us had and now have again does not come along but once in a lifetime. We realize that we each needed to experience things in life to truly appreciate each other. I cry tears of joy all of the time instead of tears of sadness.

While *The Fantasticks* certainly rings true for Lost and Found Lovers, if rekindled lovers were its only audience, it would not have survived thirty-four uninterrupted years. This was the first live theater production I ever attended, and I loved it at fourteen as much as I do today. Viewers of any age can appreciate the hopefulness and optimism that pervade the play. It conveys the message that life is really simple if we follow our hearts. Life will turn out all right at the end, and love will turn out all right at the end, despite the hardships in the middle. Successful Lost and Found Lovers demonstrate this same optimistic message, and that is why we love their stories so.

REKINDLED FILM AFFAIRS

Casablanca, one of the most beloved films in America, is a Lost and Found Love movie. Though many films produced throughout the years use exotic settings and political intrigue, the mystique of *Casablanca* remains. This is largely due to this movie's rekindled romance and the many strong emotions inherent in it— the sweet initial love in Paris, the resentments that live along with the love throughout the years, the beauty and hopefulness of the renewed relationship, and finally the poignant second parting.

Would this film have been as popular if the Lost and Found Lovers had remained together? Maybe not. Maybe we watch it over and over because we want to resolve the ending for ourselves, to "make it right," just as some Lost Love Project rekindlers tried again and again with their Lost Lovers. A sequel to this movie is planned. Will its writers dare to let these Lost and Found Lovers lose each other again?

The Lost and Found Love theme in movies has many variations. Here are some examples:

- Lost and Found Lovers Happily Reunited: *Gigi, An Affair to Remember* (and its recent remake, *Love Affair*), *Soapdish, Lifeguard, A Little Night Music, Phffft!, Doctor Zhivago, Cocktail, Grease, Map of the Human Heart, Mahogany, What's Eating Gilbert Grape, The Godfather, She Wore a Yellow Ribbon, Bambi, The Lion King, Dave, Conte d'hiver (A Tale of Winter), Don Juan DeMarco*
- Lost and Found Lovers Miserably Reunited: (None)
- Lost Lovers Rekindle the Flame, Then Part: *Casablanca, Violets Are Blue*
- Lost Lovers Rekindle, Part, Rekindle, Part, Rekindle: *When Harry Met Sally, Same Time Next Year, For the Boys, Forrest Gump*
- Rekindled Romance by Proxy: *The Favor, Clerks*

- Reason for Initial Separation: Parent(s) Disapproved of the Romance: *Les Parapluies de Cherbourg (The Umbrellas of Cherbourg), Splendor in the Grass, A Summer Place*
- Reason for Initial Separation: Federal Witness Protection Program for Fifteen Years: *Bird on a Wire*
- Reason for Initial Separation: $1 million: *Indecent Proposal*
- Reason for Initial Separation: Mistaken Ouija Board: *Only You*
- Falling in Love at Class Reunion with Lost Lover: *Spring Reunion*
- Falling in Love at Class Reunion with Lost Lover's Daughter: *Reunion*
- The Lost and Found Lovers Are Gay: *Torch Song Trilogy*
- Lost Lovers Renew Love After Death: *Ghost, Always, The Princess Bride, Chances Are, Dona Flor and Her Two Husbands, Dead Again*
- Lost Lovers Renew Love After Parting at Birth: *Made in Heaven*
- Lost and Found Marriage: *The Parent Trap, Fearless, Prêt à porter (Ready to Wear), When a Man Loves a Woman, Mr. Wonderful, The Philadelphia Story*
- Lost and Found Marriage Using Lost Lovers' Identical Twins: *The Palm Beach Story*
- Lost and Found Wife Returns after His Remarriage: *Seems Like Old Times, My Favorite Wife, Three for the Show, Move Over Darling*
- Rekindled Love by Time Machine, Magic, or Other SciFi Construct: *Forever Young, Brigadoon, Bram Stoker's Dracula, Somewhere in Time, The Time Machine, Timecop, The Little Mermaid, Big*
- Rekindled Love by Movie Sequel: *A Man and a Woman (Un Homme et une femme): 20 Years Later, Star Wars* trilogy
- Rekindled Love by Movie-in-a-Movie but Not by the Actors Making the Movie-in-a-Movie: *The French Lieutenant's Woman*
- Rekindled Love and Marriage with a Total Stranger: *Sommersby*

RENEWED ROMANCE ON THE AIRWAVES

Television has used rekindled romance as a central premise for a weekly series. A popular detective drama called *Finder of Lost Loves* starred Tony Francioso and ran from September 1984 to August 1985. (Long before that, there was a radio show with a similar name.) Each week a wealthy widower (Francioso) reunited old flames with the help of his late wife's sister and a computer named Oscar.

Lost Love is a staple for daily talk shows. Soap operas also feature renewed romances—Luke and Laura on *General Hospital,* Bo and Hope on *Days of Our Lives,* and Tad and Dixie on *All My Children.*

Many movies and miniseries made for television have featured rekindled romances. *Love Among the Ruins* (1975) starred Katharine Hepburn as a Lost Lover who renews the romance of her youth with a barrister (Sir Laurence Olivier), late in life. A newer movie (1996), *Our Son, The Matchmaker,* tells the story of a young couple who gave up a baby for adoption; years later these former sweethearts are reunited by this grown child's search—as in the stories of several Lost Love Project couples. In a lighter vein is *Bionic Everafter,* in which the Six Million Dollar Man (Lee Majors) and the Bionic Woman (Lindsay Wagner) reunite after many years off the air.

An example of a Lost and Found Love miniseries is *Scarlett,* a sequel to Margaret Mitchell's classic *Gone With the Wind.* It ends with the happy reunion of Scarlett and Rhett, along with the daughter he never knew, as they walk hand-in-hand through the lush Irish countryside. If the ending had been any different, I believe we would yearn for a sequel to the sequel.

Weekly situation comedies and dramas are always a good place to find Lost Lovers. During one season, while I was researching the Lost Love Project, more than ten weekly shows featured lost and found love, and some of these used the theme of rekindled romance more than once, involving different characters. It is significant that most of these episodes, as well as the movies and miniseries above, were aired at the time of the Nielsen ratings, also called "sweeps weeks," when the television networks try to capture the greatest number of viewers. Even my own appearance on *The Oprah Winfrey Show,* featuring the topics of first loves and rekindled romances, was originally aired as a lead-in to the Nielsen ratings.

Even more important to the networks is a series finale, which is often watched even by people who have not been regular viewers but who want to see how the show concludes. The final episode of *Cheers* was an attempted rekindled romance between Diane and Sam, and the two-hour conclusion to the series *Sisters* included the reunion of Georgie and her ex-husband.

The prominent position and timing that the networks give this topic says a lot about viewers' fascination with Lost and Found Love.

THE LOST AND FOUND LOVE HIT PARADE

Some hit songs about rekindled love are listed in Appendix I. They span a wide time period (1932 to 1995) and encompass a variety of styles, although country music generally lacks reunion songs; the few that do exist usually end with a second parting. As one fan told me, "In country, even the dawg don't come back."

In general, there are far more songs about lovers who miss their sweethearts—or songs about lovers who want another chance—than songs about those who do reunite. This surely indicates how many people would like to rekindle a romance, if only they could. The numerous happily reunited couples of the Lost Love Project certainly are proof that love can actually be renewed.

Chapter Four

AS TIME GOES BY:

LIFE STAGE LOVE LESSONS

I HAVE ALWAYS BEEN fascinated by time. Is it possible to travel back in time? Or travel forward? Can the past and future co-exist somehow, as Albert Einstein surmised, along with the present?

As a developmental psychology professor, I look at how people are changed by time. As time goes by, we develop new skills and new ways of feeling, thinking, and behaving, although we keep many aspects of our younger selves. Adults can still be childishly dependent or playful sometimes, and fiercely independent and serious on other occasions. We can still ride a bicycle in midlife, even though we first learned to do so when we were six. We can go back to school in our seventies or fall in love in our eighties. The lessons of childhood and adolescence remain with us, even though we have matured beyond those early years, gaining knowledge along the way.

Many psychologists believe that the issues we face in adulthood are really the same problems we faced much earlier in life. They cycle back to reappear in slightly different, more mature forms across later stages of development. We do not really "move on"; we "build on." In the words of a popular expression, "The more things change, the more they stay the same."

Some of these developmental issues continue to influence our love relationships. In this chapter we will explore how these aspects of normal maturation might explain the compelling forces underlying Lost and Found Love. Our developmental history predisposes us to want to renew relationships. And you will see that, in these rekindled romances at least, the past and future *do* coexist with the present.

CHILDHOOD: FEELING, BEHAVING, AND THINKING

Babies are born with the capacity to love, but they do not yet have a focus for that attachment. This develops slowly over the first year of life. They begin by focusing attention on their environment, which includes the people who touch them, play with them, talk to them, and feed them.

Feeling

In the last half of their first year, children develop a fear of strangers called *stranger anxiety*. It is a normal part of development, not a problem. In fact, this "anxiety" can be seen to be good, because to have a fear of strangers, the baby must have developed a self concept ("This person is different from me") and must have come to value significant people ("This person is different from Mommy"). Even though stranger anxiety begins to subside after the first birthday, we never completely lose our anxiety about meeting new people, or about being in new situations. This wariness remains a positive emotion, because it can protect our safety. One woman in the Lost Love Project stated this very directly:

> SOMETIMES I THINK MY LOST Lover was "put back" into my life when I needed him the most. Just knowing he's there has helped me deal with a lot of issues—like my divorce, and all the emotional turmoil that goes with it. The familiarity of him is such a comfort to me. I *know* him. The idea of having to start dating strangers used to make me nauseous.

When we apply this aspect of childhood development to rekindled romance, we realize that the comfortable feelings experienced by these reunited couples hark back not only to the time they first met, but also to the ongoing struggle with stranger anxiety that began in their first year. These lovers are not strangers to each other; in an earlier time they represented comfort and security—they became familiar, like Mommy and Home. One woman expressed her refound comfort this way:

I LEFT MY CHILDHOOD HOME as a teenager and never went back. Last summer, however, I reconnected with my Lost Lover. He's given me a peaceful and secure sense of reconnection to my childhood. This is an adventure filled with joy and promise.

When I was a child, I would eat a cupcake from the bottom up, saving the intensely sweet icing to savor at the last. Perhaps I am living my life—after all its past disappointments and traumas—that way, too.

A similar emotion that appears at the end of a baby's first year is *separation anxiety,* the fear that arises when the caretaker is not present. Psychoanalyst Bruno Bettelheim calls this fear that we will be left all alone "man's greatest fear," and with good reason: An infant who is not protected will die. Fairy tales such as Hansel and Gretel, Jack and the Beanstalk, and Snow White, as well as the *Wizard of Oz* series, play on this fear. Because of it, writes Bettelheim, "the ultimate consolation is that we shall never be deserted." This was the consolation that a number of the Lost Love Project participants offered to their Lost and Found Lovers, pledging love unto death, and thereafter as well. One man wrote to express his unending devotion to his sweetheart:

FORTY-FIVE YEARS PASSED BEFORE I saw my loved one again. I called her, and you know the rest. We are now into our eleventh year of bewitchment.

When we are ready for rocking chairs on my front porch, I want more than anything to take her hand, look into her eyes, and see the face of the woman I fell in love with so many years ago.

Where we end up after death, only God knows. But we will surely be together.

When Lost and Found Love results in a second abandonment, it feels especially devastating, as one man described:

IN MY BEDROOM IS A gold-framed picture of my Lost Lover and me, back together after thirty-eight years. The day I first met her is still so vivid to me. A buddy said I just had to follow him to the beach and meet this beautiful girl. Within minutes, I was sharing a corner of her towel. Everything was perfect.

Over the next few weeks, I got my mother's '59 Pontiac, and my Lost Lover and I were inseparable. We'd park in front of her house, kiss, grope, and get down on that vast bench seat in that huge Pontiac and go at it some more. We were so in love, and in those days innocent and pure.

After that summer, she went off to college and I joined the Navy. My life just evolved after that, and I honestly didn't think much about Fran. I was living in California then. But sometime after my first marriage ended, I was at Newark Airport, on my way to Manhattan chasing after some girl. I realized I wasn't far from Asbury Park where her family once lived. Hell, why not? So I drove to Asbury. Her dad told me she was married and happy, so I left it alone.

The eighties saw another marriage come and go. I had a successful career in television. I had an Emmy, a Porsche . . . and a big empty house. I was visiting a friend one day and met his brother from . . . ta da! . . . Asbury Park. That must have rattled some brain cells, because the next week I called this brother to get the address of Fran's dad's accounting firm. The ol' man had passed away, but I got Fran's address. She sat on my letter for about a month, then wrote back. She was divorced. After that, we talked for two or three hours a night. God, I've never had such chemistry over the phone!

I soon visited and we fell madly in love. It was so rich, so wonderful, so perfect. Everything we did was a blast. Driving down to her mother's place, I asked her to marry me, and she accepted. I nearly wrecked the rental car, my eyes were tearing up so.

But I made a few mistakes . . . and boy, did it cost me!

I quit my job, sold my house, and headed back east to live with Fran. She spent her mornings jogging, a few laps in a pool, then off to work. After work she hit the gym, ate a few bean sprouts, vacuumed, and put in two loads of laundry before bed. Meanwhile, I didn't have any job prospects, and my clothes were still in the guest closet. I had to share a bathroom with her kids.

My depression was soon rolling in, right along with the shore fog. One day I woke up with chest pains. I went into panic mode. I packed my stuff into my car and left without even leaving a note. I cried all the way back to Santa Monica. I wasn't "mentally together" enough to tell Fran I was in a crisis. I destroyed her trust in me. I spent four weeks in bed, watching the boob tube: twelve on, twelve off.

Then I called her. I blithered. I sobbed. But she hated me for doing that to her. I found out that *abandonment* is her big issue. That was our last contact.

Separation anxiety appears and peaks approximately two months after stranger anxiety. It, too, is a normal part of development and indicates that the child has formed an attachment to the caretaker. In fact, children who lacked a primary caretaker in their early months may not demonstrate separation anxiety, and its absence may be a sign of psychological trouble.

Attachment is the beginning of the bond that we call love. Gradually separation anxiety subsides as the child learns something new: Mommy comes back. Children can then use this comforting knowledge when they are anxious about being separated from other people, places, and things they love. One woman in the Lost Love Project found her way back to her country of origin and to a lost friend—from her toddler days:

I AM TWENTY-SEVEN YEARS OLD now, and I was born in South Africa. When I was twelve, my parents immigrated to America, bringing me and my two brothers. It was hard for me to leave the familiar places and friends! When I was fifteen, I returned home alone for a short visit to South Africa, for no apparent reason. I simply felt a strong need to return, and I couldn't resist the pull. So I went back only to fall madly in love with my older brother's best friend. I had known him since I was three years old.

He was sixteen at this time. We couldn't deny how deeply in love we were with each other. Knowing I was to leave soon, we decided to enjoy my entire six-week trip together, vowing to find each other one day and promising never to forget the magical love we shared.

Well, time passed and after many years of waiting for him, I finally moved on in life and married another man at twenty-two, still secretly loving my Lost Lover in my heart. When my marriage turned abusive, I filed for divorce. A few months later my Lost Lover did come looking for me. I was skeptical at first, but we met again and yes, magically fell in love all over again—this time as adults. We both felt we had never stopped loving each other and the love we had this time was definitely based on our past love for each other.

We have now been together for four years and are happily married. We have definitely been through our share of rough roads, but we feel our love was based on such a strong bond from the past that this is what has helped keep us close.

We are very attracted to each other and have great passion together. We have discovered and developed the most wonderful love imaginable. We have something very special, true soul mates who have lost and found each other again!

Separation anxiety, like stranger anxiety, is never fully resolved. No matter what age we reach, we do not like separating from those we love. So the endings of romantic relationships always bring pain. One man wrote about the end of his initial romance and about his Lost Lover's reaction:

ALL DURING HER GROWING-UP YEARS, my Lost Lover was taught never to show her feelings. So she looked cool as a cucumber when we broke up. I saw this as a confirmation that she had only been playing with my emotions, that I was the only one with a broken heart. I learned almost forty years later that she secretly cried long and hard in her bedroom for months.

Neither of us realized at the time the huge significance of this seemingly childish breakup to both our lives. Naturally, our parents viewed this sort of thing as puppy love, trivial, plenty more fish in the sea, that sort of thing. I am here forty-five years later to affirm that it wasn't trivial.

When Lost Lovers return to rekindle the romance, it can be felt as a tremendous relief. As one Lost Love Project participant wrote:

OUR WEDDING DAY WAS THE most wonderful day of our lives. Everything was perfect, even the weather. I know I was the most ecstatically happy woman on earth that day. It is difficult to put into words the incredible joy we shared on our wedding day. Joining together after such a long time, and after I thought our chance had slipped away, I felt incredibly overjoyed and *relieved* at the same time.

Those we love, and from whom we are separated, are supposed to return. That is the foundation of our sense of security, and we learned it before our first birthdays. The return of the Lost Lover makes the world seem right, so the romance seems right—as it very often is.

Behaving

Harry F. Harlow, a past president of the American Psychological Association, studied the bond between mother and baby in rhesus monkeys. After being apart from a terry cloth substitute mother for six months, and then reuniting, the baby monkeys demonstrated much more than just relief. They bolted over barriers to get to "her"; they ran around fearful stimuli to reach "her"; they clutched and clung to "her" for hours. This exaggerated need to reach and touch the surrogate mother indicated that instead of being weakened by time apart, the attachment had been strengthened.

Extensive research on attachment bonds between human children and their mothers indicates that an *insecure attachment* (like that in the Harlow monkey study) might very well result in clinging behavior when the mother and baby are reunited.

These studies might in part explain why emotions and behaviors in rekindled romances are so much more intense than in new relationships. Of course there is relief and intense joy at having a loved one back again. But the separation itself has probably caused an attachment—an insecure attachment—that produces this anxious need to touch. One woman described her reunion:

> I MET HIM AT THE airport, and we spent five of the most precious days of our lives together and realized we still and always have loved each other. I know I will never forget those five days. Seeing him for the first time after fifteen years was incredible. We just held each other for the first few hours!

Thinking

X   Babies learn about their world at the same time that they learn the language to describe that world. But when learning a second language, a child or adult already views the world through the earlier, native language, and relies on that first language to understand sentences in the new language. In other words, a translation and a comparison are made.

Our tendency to consider the first thing learned as the most genuine and comfortable, and the second thing as something that we can evaluate only by comparing to the original, is not lost after we learn language. A first love—the person with whom we learn about love and actually create what love means—will be the standard at the beginning of any subsequent relationship, until we gain comfort with the new loved one. If we have a chance to rekindle the flame with that first lover, even if later loves were long and happy, we suddenly find ourselves on comfortable ground, speaking again in our "native language" of romance. As one woman wrote:

IT WAS SO EASY TO reestablish an old relationship, as if we'd never been apart. We laughed and said it was comfortable, like an old pair of slippers—no nervousness, no head games, passion was greater, we felt blessed. We could be ourselves. I could get down on the floor and roll with the dog and not feel stupid.

Jean Piaget—a Swiss biologist and naturalist who pioneered research on how children think—found that when children are about seven years old, they develop the concept of *reversibility*. They realize that a rule or process can be reversed to put something back into its original form: numbers that are added together can be subtracted again; a ball of clay that has been stretched into a sausage can be rolled into a ball again; and water poured from one container into another can be poured back. Later on in adulthood, if a Lost Lover returns, the couple who parted have reversed the separation; the two people subtracted have been re-added. Given our developmental conditioning, this process seems only right.

———— ※ ————

ADOLESCENCE: SELF, PEERS, PARENTS

Adolescence is considered to begin with puberty and end in the early twenties, when a person can consistently take social and emotional responsibility for his or her life. Since most of the Lost Love Project participants were teenagers when their romances began, they passed through the tasks of their adolescence together.

Self

Psychoanalyst Erik H. Erikson believed that the main task of the adolescent period is to find an identity. An adolescent's self concept is ideally an integration of childhood gains with recent body changes, logical thought, and social skill development with friends of both sexes, as well as trial-and-error learning. The adolescent sweethearts have forged large parts of their identities together, much as siblings do in early childhood.

Adolescents lean heavily on their peers for developing a self concept. A boyfriend or girlfriend is even more influential—especially for learning what it means to be masculine or feminine in our society. A breakup between teenagers causes a wound to the self. That is one reason why adolescents are often devastated by these partings, and they do not understand how their parents can minimize their loss.

Adolescent sweethearts will use that first romance as the model for romances that follow. Anthropologist Helen Fisher, author of *Anatomy of Love,* refers to this model as our "love map," a "template for ideal sweethearts." In an interview in *Good Housekeeping,* Fisher added, "So it doesn't surprise me that we go back to that person again." One Lost Love Project participant observed:

> WE WERE ALL FRIENDS. KATHY was dating Ralph and me at the same time. She chose to marry Ralph, a marriage that lasted sixteen years. Seven years after Ralph died, Kathy and I remet, dated, and married. That was eight years ago.
>
> Since the ninth grade, *she* is the standard by which I have measured every other woman in my life. *It's great!*

When romantic events happen for the first time—the first date, the first slow dance, the first kiss, the first "I love you"—the arousal teenagers feel, perhaps heightened by the adrenaline rush of insecurity, is momentous and unforgettable. In some cases it will become matchless. One man wrote about his early love feelings:

> MY LOST LOVER AND I are both American Indians. When we were young, our families both lived on the same reservation.
>
> When I was fifteen, I went to a dance with my buddy. I was very shy, but he dragged me onto the dance floor and introduced me to Sue. She turned to me and gave me what became known to her and me as "The Look." My eyes told me that she was interested! My brain had a mental cramp, my tongue went on strike, my heart jumped, my stomach got butterflies, and my feet were pasted to the floor.
>
> She said thirty years later that the feelings were the same for her.

If you've ever had that happen to you when you first met someone—and I'm sure it can happen only once in a lifetime—then you know what it's like. If it has not happened to you, there is no way to really explain it.

We don't remember too much about that first night together. We know that even though there was a band and a lot of people there, everyone but Sue and I just disappeared.

We were first "everythings" to each other. After that First Look, she and I had our First Crush, which of course led to our First Kiss. That turned into our First Puppy Love. From there came our First French Kiss, then our First Experiments with our bodies. That grew into our First (and really only) Love, and then we became First Lovers. No, this didn't all happen on our First Night!

If a chance comes years later to try again with this person—to "right the wrong" and heal the self concept of the one who was rejected, or to relieve the other's guilt and correct the mistake—the situation is emotionally loaded.

Over the years, our memory of the actual details of the romance becomes distorted as we magnify the happiness we felt and forget the pain. No real being can compete with remembered perfection—except maybe the Lost Lover in person.

Peers

A teenager's peer group offers a supportive haven for trying out new roles away from the judgments of adults. It serves as a very influential Greek chorus, giving feedback to each friend in turn about the suitability of a current sweetheart and the solutions to romantic conflicts. This role falls especially on the best friend, with whom double-dating and the most personal confidences are shared. But a best friend is not objective, as this young woman found out:

I MET MY LOST LOVER in 1984 at a high school football game. We fell completely in love, even though I was only sixteen. He made me feel special, and we spent a lot of time with our families. I was proud to go places with him, and he called me his "One and Only." I thought things were perfect, and I never thought anything would ever come between us.

Unfortunately, friends can put a lot of pressure on a person, especially a sixteen-year-old. So I let my best friend convince me I shouldn't tie myself to one person. As a result, I told my Lost Lover I wanted to be free. Right after that, I missed him so much, even though I went on to date someone new.

A few years ago, this girlfriend got in touch with me again after years of no contact. Over the next few months, my Lost Lover came up in one of our conversations. She finally told me why she was so adamant that I break up with him. She said she was jealous of the time I was spending with him, because it was taking away time from her. She knew I'd need her if I broke up with him, and the rest is history.

As adolescents search for identity, they must become individuals, separate even from friends. Maturing adolescents want conformity, but they do not want to be clones. Thus friendships can be volatile, and romances, requiring compromise and some merging of identities, can bloom and end quickly. This is another reason why some Lost and Found Lovers parted when they were teenagers. One teen might want individuation while the other needs intimacy. The following story arrived from Montreal, from a man in his mid-forties:

AS A TEENAGER, I WAS the classic geek. Tall, gangly, clumsy, with glasses and bad teeth, who wouldn't have known what to do with a girl if she were spread out nude on a platter. But my best friend invited me to a movie, and he brought a girl along. I fell in love with her instantly. She was very pretty, but like me: shy and timid, just blending into the background.

A few days later, at school, I saw her being hassled by a couple of jocks, and I sort of stepped in and told the guys to get lost. They looked at me, trying to decide whether to punch me out or laugh. Luckily they chose laughter, walking away saying, "They deserve each other." Carol and I became immediate friends, spending lunch times together, and walks after school.

When I finally proclaimed my love for her two years later, she told me she only loved me as a friend or a big brother. I was crushed, but told her I could wait until she formed a different opinion. But I had no time; she soon moved with her family to Europe.

I wrote countless letters, and visited her there. Then back to Canada and the letters. One day she wrote to tell me she was coming to Canada to see her married sister. I was ecstatic . . . but she showed up with a baby! She was raising the baby alone, because the guy left them, and her parents disowned her. I told her I still loved her and would take care of her if she would have me. She said no, that things had changed.

I went home and burned all the letters and photos, anything that reminded me of her. Or so I thought!

Twenty years went by, and she still tormented my dreams. I never married. I just had short romances to fill the lonely void in my heart. Finally I sought therapy, and the doctor told me to try to find her and put the past to rest. I was able to trace her through her twenty-year-old address.

Very cautiously I wrote a letter to see if she remembered me. Four days later, I got a call and there she was! She was so happy she was crying, and asked me why I would bother with someone who had broken my heart years ago. Holding back tears, I reminded her that I told her I would never replace her, and I kept my promise.

We will be married in the fall. Very rarely in life do you ever get a second chance at correcting a mistake made in one's youth. And you can count on one fact: that nothing in this world short of death is going to prevent me from getting the happiness out of life I was denied so long ago.

I will close by saying to always believe and pursue your dreams. Please wish me luck!

Parents

One important finding of the Lost Love Project is that the most common reason these teenage romances ended was that the parents disapproved. The children did as they were told and broke up with their loved ones. Despite the common belief that teenagers are by definition rebellious, clearly there is not rebellion in every home or in every teen. One young woman who ended her initial romance with her Lost Lover because of her mother's disapproval, rekindled her romance five years later when she was on her own (though still a teen):

MY HUSBAND AND I FIRST met when I was thirteen and he was eighteen. We dated for a couple of weeks. Because of my mother protecting her daughter, we hardly saw each other, so we broke up. We didn't see each other for five years.

Then one day our paths crossed. It just so happened that he was looking for me, to see how I was doing. There was this tent ministry in a park, and he just had a feeling I would be there. So he went every day for the week it was there. He asked everyone there if they had seen me. He knew I was a Christian and that I was involved with my church. On the last day I went there. He was about to give up and go home when he saw me. He was so excited and happy that he finally found me. A couple days later we decided to give our relationship another chance. I was then eighteen and independent, having just graduated from high school.

A year later we were married. That was three years ago. We are planning to have a baby soon. We are in love now more than ever and we keep loving each other more every day.

Adolescent sons or daughters may look mature and may even be taller than their parents, so it is easy to expect them to think rationally, like adults. But they cannot always do so. A significant characteristic of teenagers is that they see themselves as more important than they are. Psychologist David Elkind called this *adolescent egocentrism*. The teen is not choosing to be selfish and self-centered, but is merely going through a normal stage of thought development. Adolescent egocentrism sometimes prevents teens from recognizing useful advice that their parents offer. They believe that only they have had these experiences or felt these feelings. Elkind explains that it is not surprising for a girl to say, "But Mother, you don't know how it feels to be in love." Considering the number of couples in the Lost Love Project who did listen to their parents rather than to their hearts and did end their romances, then happily reunited years later, perhaps that girl is right.

Another aspect of egocentrism is what Elkind called the *personal fable,* when adolescents imagine themselves as being heroic or mythic. Their belief in the uniqueness of their feelings, together with this heroic component, magnifies their sense of the romance. The fairy tales and conventions of love in the media, with which we grow up, embellish their love with images of dashing knights and fair ladies. When Lost and Found Lovers have shared these images as teenagers, they are wont to describe their reunited love as "our unique story" and "just like a fairy tale." A middle-aged woman wrote to me from California:

I INITIALLY MET MY LOST Lover when I was a few days short of my sixteenth birthday. "Sweet Sixteen and never been kissed" was an obsessive thought. I wanted to be kissed.

But my mother went ballistic when I turned up with this boy, because he was Mexican-American. We sneak-dated for years with the help of my friends. But I could not face a lifetime of having him constantly run down by my mother, so I eventually left him.

I married. But the love I still had for my first love was literally a seven-year ache. Only the birth of my twin daughters and the accompanying mother-love intensity displaced him.

When he called years later, the reunion packed quite an emotional wallop! I became attuned to the medieval cult of courtly love: loving someone outside of marriage. I heard love songs in a new light. I was lovesick, with obsessive thoughts and dreams about him. I had trouble sleeping, and I lost fifteen pounds. It was Lenten season: lessons on death and resurrection. The reunion brought new life into me.

I know you need clear-cut results for statistical analysis, and yet I am emotionally rambling, I don't know why. But I come from a cynical, unsentimental family, in contrast to the venting that I am doing right now. My mother's refrain—"I don't understand you"—haunts me. So maybe I am writing because—yes, that's it!—Nancy Kalish understands.

And a woman, now in her thirties, expressed herself this way:

SOMETIMES WHEN THEY'RE YOUNG, EITHER because of what others say or just because of youthful self-doubt, people don't feel they can trust their feelings—they believe that they are "too young." I know now that what I felt for my Lost Lover was indeed love. I am now married to the best friend I've ever had and am as happy as I've ever hoped to be. It's a real-life fairy tale!

EARLY ADULTHOOD: OLD THINKING AND NEW BEHAVING

Young adulthood ranges approximately from the twenties to thirty or thirty-five years of age. During these years, people retain some adolescent thinking patterns, but they are faced with life decisions—marriage, children, career, and finances—that often demand maturity and wisdom beyond their experience. It should not be surprising, then, that people make decisions in early adulthood that they may regard as mistakes when they are older. Their reasoning abilities lag behind their need to adopt adult behaviors.

Old Thinking

Young adults still think that life is limitless, that the number of potential love partners is limitless, and that they themselves are limitless. And so they forge ahead with feelings of omnipotence that remain from their adolescence. Now, however, the stakes are higher: Young adults are no longer under their parents' protective wings, and they must take risks and make decisions that might take years to modify or correct. Choosing incompatible love partners—or breaking up with viable love partners—during these years is a common cause of regret later in life.

The majority of Lost Love Project participants acknowledged that their bad judgments about romance during young adulthood caused them to make mistakes in their rekindled romance history. Usually the mistake took the form of letting go of the Lost Lover initially, but sometimes the mistake was in the choice of that partner in the first place. One woman in her twenties shared this story:

I ARRIVED IN CANADA AS a permanent resident from East Asia, and met my Lost Lover shortly after my arrival. A few months later we became engaged. He was a newly arrived refugee from Iran. My parents were obviously not pleased with my decision. They wanted me to return home immediately and continue my education. They absolutely hated my fiancé.

I told them I would go to law school and they sent me money. However, my Lost Lover and I opened a business with their money instead. Two years later, my parents paid me a surprise visit. When they saw I was not in school, I had to choose between them and my Lost Lover. I chose my Lost Lover, and I haven't been able to talk to my parents since.

I helped him to become a permanent resident. Shortly after that, he convinced me to sell the business and move to Alberta. I requested a job transfer, but for several months he was living in Alberta and I was still in Montreal. I found out he was not investing the money from the sale of the business, and he was using my credit cards uncontrollably. When he used up all our credit and cash, he said he wanted out. He even took what valuables we had. Since we were not married and all the cards were in my name, there was not much I could do except declare bankruptcy.

I was in so much pain! I felt so betrayed and hated myself for not listening to my parents! I went back to college and turned to prayer to help me forget my anguish. I was unable to have any relationships after that.

Then my Lost Lover called me. He talked about his life after me, and I felt so sorry for him that it did not seem to matter what he had done to me. For a few months, I comforted him and helped him financially. The first time I saw him, I cried for hours. I thought we had another chance.

But one day I tried to call him. Number not in service anymore; he was gone again. But I don't hate him. I think he did me a favor by coming around the second time. He freed me from all my heartaches and fantasies. And my past is past. The important thing is my future and the inner peace I finally found. I can move on.

New Behaving

Key events often occur during early adulthood—getting married, renting a first apartment, buying a house, beginning a career, or having a child—but there is wide variation. A twenty-to-thirtysomething peer group could include some people who are married without children, some married with children, some not yet married, and some already divorced. This variation in early adulthood behavior is evident in the Lost Love Project: Some couples met for the first time in their twenties and reunited many years later, while others in their twenties were already reuniting with a Lost Lover from five or more years earlier.

Early adulthood is generally a time of "acquiring." People change jobs, move from place to place, and change friends from new to newer. And because they have only just escaped the parental restrictions of adolescence, they still feel insecure about whether "real grownups"—their parents and people who are their parents' age—consider them adults. They often deal with their insecurity by putting as much distance as possible between themselves and their childhood: They think they have outgrown their old friends, hometowns, and interests. People in their twenties and thirties are still busy rejecting their roots and cannot yet look at the past—and past relationships—with nostalgia. For this reason, most of the renewed romances in the Lost Love Project took place after early adulthood.

MIDDLE ADULTHOOD: CHOICE, CHANGE, AND COMFORT

Middle adulthood, ages thirty-five to sixty or sixty-five, can bring its own storms and stresses. Psychologist Daniel Levinson conducted interviews with middle-aged men and notes in his well-known book, *The Seasons of a Man's Life,* that in midlife, many men feel restricted at work and at home and might be tempted to rebel. Even if nothing changes in a man's external life, internal changes can make a man view his life differently.

Similarly, Roger Gould, psychologist and author of the research study *Transformations: Growth and Change in Adult Life,* found that "adulthood is not a plateau; rather it is a dynamic and changing time for all of us." He believes that we begin to feel stuck with too much responsibility in our thirties and develop a sense of urgency when we reach our forties and realize just how limited life is. Moreover, unfinished business of childhood returns and requires introspection and change.

Choice

Erik Erikson referred to middle adulthood as the time of choosing between *generativity* or *stagnation:* Either we choose the risky but growth-oriented path leading us to create, produce, and reproduce, or we stay on the safe but growth-stifling path that allows us to remain the same.

In some cases, by middle adulthood, people must face the reality that what they envisioned for themselves when they were younger did not materialize, or that they have not achieved their goals. The choices are to feel perpetually disappointed, to accept what one does have, or to make the changes necessary to reach the original goals.

When middle-aged adults choose to change their careers or marriages, they are often stigmatized by the traditional explanation: a midlife crisis. If changes seem to have been made quickly, friends and family might see them as an ill-conceived quest to retain one's youth. But actually such change is often an act of courage, providing an opportunity for growth and for a deeper happiness during the years to follow. Roger Gould's hypothesis about the feeling of urgency in these years—the belief that one's time is limited—explains the rapid decision making and the changes that are incomprehensible to others.

Many of the Lost Love Project participants divorced during these years and reunited with their Lost Lovers. Some first reconnected with the Lost Lovers and then decided to divorce their spouses. Others chose to remain married and hide their involvement with the former sweethearts. Whatever the order or method, many of these Lost and Found Lovers described being influenced by the midlife tasks of looking back at one's life, evaluating old goals against current reality, and choosing to make changes as necessary. As one man stated on his Lost Love Project questionnaire, "I no longer had the time to waste in a bad marriage, or any more years to be without her."

In other cases, people meet their career goals in middle age. The hard work and obsessively long hours of the early years begin to pay off in status and financial security. They find new time for leisure and for reassessing their priorities. One man pursued a Lost and Found Love with his newly available time:

> WHEN MY LOST LOVER AND I broke up at age twenty-one, I was really devastated. However, it gave me time to focus on my professional career and grow both professionally and personally. Had we not broken up back then, the relationship would not have survived. During the interim, I remained single, dated, and worked seventy to eighty hours a week consistently.
>
> When she called years later, the little flame absolutely ignited. She had just separated, we moved in together, and one day after her divorce we were married. We will be celebrating our fifteenth anniversary this year.

Change

Some changes in midlife occur without a choice. At a time when adolescents are going through many physical changes that require psychological adjustments, and want sympathy for a pimple or a "bad hair" day, their middle-aged parents are experiencing their own physical changes (which they see as much more traumatic, of course). These include weight gain, the first pair of eyeglasses, menopause, diminished sexual drive, wrinkles, aches and pains, high blood pressure, and other ailments which create a panicky feeling that they have become just like their parents, in addition to strange bouts of acne not experienced since junior high, and gray hair days—or no hair days! Rekindled romance, however, is blind to these changes, as one woman's story illustrates:

WE MET ON NEW YEAR'S EVE when I was a waitress at a country/western nightclub. I danced with the customers, and more and more frequently this gentleman became my partner. When the magical midnight hour arrived and everyone began the traditional kissing, he was right there. One particularly passionate kiss resulted in our belts becoming hooked together. Mine broke in an attempt to disengage them. The die was cast.

We saw each other often after that, for months, but one day something changed for me. I guess I just needed space. I left him for someone else. I didn't hear from him again.

I got married but he still drifted through my thoughts more often than I care to admit. I divorced, remarried, and divorced again. Almost twenty years passed. One day, curiosity got the better of me and I went to our old stomping grounds. I picked up the local phone directory to see if his former employer knew anything about him. Within the first few words he said, "Bill is back here working and has been looking all over for you!" My heart nearly jumped out of my chest. When I heard his voice it was like the years melted away.

But my fears intensified, because I had been a slim, attractive young woman. Now I was in my mid-forties, and had gained a considerable amount of weight. He sensed my hesitancy, I told him why, and his response wiped the fear away. He said that it wasn't my size he had fallen in love with and that unless something about my personality had changed, the outer change meant nothing to him. He was true to his words!

We began where we left off, and we married. We are now beginning yet another phase of our life together, retirement. I tend the garden and he tends the horses, and together we will ride off into the sunset. By the way, I've never lost that weight and he has never uttered one word about my size.

Marital satisfaction for those who married in their twenties and thirties often declines in middle adulthood. Children might be leaving home, creating "empty nest" issues of identity and a need to rebuild the marriage partnership, or a single parent's social life, without their company. And, unfortunately, it is not uncommon in these years for friends, or one's spouse, to die. One woman reported struggling with her feelings about her terminally ill husband:

MY HUSBAND WAS DIAGNOSED A few years ago with cancer. We have four children. One day recently, I heard the news I thought I would never hear: My Lost Lover was getting a divorce. I got up the nerve to call his mother (who knows I am married and that my husband is sick) and ask for his number.

I called him, and we met several times over the next few months. I told him I felt I was still in love with him, and that if I ever become single that I wanted to resume our romance. He felt it was wrong for us to even be friends while I was married.

I think of him every day and wonder what could be if I were free. When my husband first became sick, I was terrified, but now I feel guilty because I know that his death could be the beginning of a whole new life for me.

Another problem middle-aged adults might face is that their aging parents begin to need financial, emotional, or physical care. This situation brought more than a few Lost Lovers back to their hometowns and to each other again. One woman told of her experience with this:

MY MOTHER HAD HIP REPLACEMENT surgery and I came home to take care of her when she got out of the hospital. While at home, I went out to the old homestead where my brother still lives and went through the attic to sort through a lot of old things. I found a picture of my Lost Lover in an old trunk—his graduation picture that I had when we were dating forty years ago. I sat there and thought about him and wondered what had become of him. I also had an old diary. I started to read it. It was a five-year diary I started in the eighth grade. The last entry of the diary said simply, "George and I broke up today."

So one evening I asked my mother if she knew anything about George. She told me he lived in Iowa, divorced with children and grandchildren. I got his address from his aunt and wrote him a letter. He called me! He was tickled to death to hear from me. We began talking every day, then writing and exchanging pictures. I finally decided to fly out and meet him. We hit it right off.

Now we are living in Iowa, happy as larks together. It is two years since we fell in love all over again. All because of Mom's operation.

The death of an adult child's parents led a number of Lost and Found Lovers back together. One man shared his story about this:

WE FIRST MET WHEN I was fifteen and she was fourteen. Our parents had nearby vacation lake cabins, half a mile apart. Our "dating" only occurred on weekends or long holidays, when our parents took us to the lake. It was never anything more than hugging, kissing, and long walks holding hands. We wrote to each other a great deal, but long distance phone calls back then were still uncommon.

I was from a big city, a top high school athlete, and got a football scholarship for college. The pressures on me from others caused a great strain on our long distance relationship, and I eventually broke up with her. There was no anger. We parted as friends. We went our separate ways, married, and had no contact for twenty-seven years.

Then I received the news that her father had passed away, and without hesitation I left to attend the funeral eight hundred miles away. Five years later, by chance, we were on short vacations at the lake, in our separate cabins. She learned of my mother's death and drove over to my cabin to leave a condolence note. We hugged hello, talked of family and said good-bye. But one week later we began to exchange letters and learned that we were both in divorce proceedings. Our relationship has grown ever since.

We are now totally devoted to each other, and we will be together the rest of our lives. I have never experienced anything more wonderful, nor has she. We must have truly bonded in a soulful way thirty-three years ago. It originally started at the lake, and it was rekindled there, thirty-three years later!

Not all change, of course, is negative. Middle-aged adults have gained the wisdom and experience to avoid mistakes by thinking first instead of acting impulsively. If they are willing to be introspective, the reward of finally knowing themselves can lessen chronic depression, anxiety, or dysfunctional lifestyles and free them to move on. Maturity brings patience, empathy, security, and communication skills (to name but a few of its gifts) for solving problems that could have broken up their teen relationships. In addition, an empty nest can free parents to develop other aspects of themselves.

Comfort

Considering the physical and situational changes of midlife, it is easy to understand why middle-aged adults would relish reconnecting with Lost and Found Lovers—people who see them as just as sexy and youthful as they once were. These retro romances represent a stable and comfortable connection to one's roots: the familiar places, valued objects, shared activities, and special people, even though the actual things and people may be long gone. One widow stated:

I WAS ALREADY DATING MY husband-to-be when I initially met my Lost Lover. We dated secretly then. He was not aggressive enough about our relationship and I married my husband.

I received a letter from my Lost Lover a few weeks after my husband died, although he was unaware of my husband's death. It was nice to be able to talk about the past, and the renewal of our romance allowed me to have a safe, secret, sexual relationship and still be seen as a "widow." It also restored some self-confidence in my later "date-ability."

But I can see now that in choosing to marry my husband instead of the Lost Lover, I made the right decision. And I no longer have illusions about what might have been.

Psychologically healthy adults feel like "grownups" by this time. This sense of security permits nostalgia to creep in. Midlife is a time to listen to the golden oldies radio station, to purchase the sports car that cost too much "back then," to buy back the lost dolls, trains, or books of childhood (now insultingly sold in "antiques" stores), to travel back to the extended family in the old hometown— and to search for old friends and Lost Lovers. One man in his fifties described these feelings:

WE WERE HIGH SCHOOL SWEETHEARTS. I was very much in love with her and had all sorts of future plans that included both of us. Her father knew that "cooler heads" would prevail and if we married in the future, it would be with his blessings. But her mother had a completely different idea and forced our separation in our senior year. We were both devastated by this turn of events, and lost each other for thirty years.

I have thought of her constantly in recent years. For example, I drove across the country and stood on the rim of the Grand Canyon, absorbed in its magnificent beauty, and it wasn't two minutes before my Lost Lover entered my mind. I thought how beautiful it would be to have her there with me gazing into the canyon.

I have always thought of her, over the thirty years, particularly around her birthday, or on Thanksgiving or Christmas or New Year's Eve. Anything that had to do with a family gathering would trigger vivid recollections of my Lost Lover and what might have been, if only!

I am a police officer. I spent countless hours in front of teletype machines and computer terminals searching for her all over the country. Little did I know that she was living not ten miles from my home!

I found her eventually through a thirtieth-year high school class reunion directory. I have since visited her and we have totally fallen in love with each other again. I don't know what the final results of your project will indicate, but I for one am very happy over being reunited with my Lost Lover.

Many forty- or fifty-year-old parents have children who are adolescents. These teens begin to date, attend a prom, spend endless telephone time with someone special, or fall in love. Middle-aged parents cannot help recalling their own adolescent romantic struggles as they watch their children grow up. A question may keep invading conscious thought: "I wonder what became of . . ." As one fifty-year-old man related:

MY OWN SEVENTEEN-YEAR-OLD DAUGHTER HAD an unfortunate affair of the heart recently, and I began wondering what in the world I did to my Lost Lover, that poor girl I knew when we were high schoolers so long ago. Could I have been the one in the wrong? I had to know. I had to find out.

Even leisure takes on a different, and more appreciated, significance in mid-life. People develop new skills and hobbies, diversify old interests, travel, play, and relax. Our partners in leisure, our friends, change from those of our earlier years, when they were mostly other parents of young children. People in middle adulthood tend to socialize less and to favor a few old friends. When asked to name a best friend, they often cite someone from a past place of residence. This echoes the middle adulthood theme of looking to the past, to those we once held dear, and maybe to that one special person who might become a Lost and

Found Lover. One woman, coming to terms with family losses, expressed this well:

I HAVE SINCE MOVED IN with my daughter. We've had a lot of time to talk, to cry, to make sense of the tragedy. The one most important thing I've come up with is that you never know where life is going to take you, so you'd better take stock of what you have while it is here. Forget old grudges, tell your friends and loved ones how you feel about them, clear up unfinished business, live today.

That is what I decided to do with my Lost Lover. Even though twenty-five years passed, I still felt a huge regret over having lost my first real love for all those years. I wanted to say that I am sorry, that I was such a jerk. And I always wondered if he ever thought about me.

LATE ADULTHOOD: REVIEW AND RENEW

The later years continue the process of reviewing and synthesizing the various aspects of one's life. This process may occur in dreams or in the waking state, as random memories or as continuous and highly visual images of the past. Reviewing the past helps people resolve old guilt and fear, or reconnect with estranged relatives and former friends. Such reconnections bring a sense of completion, and thus comfort, toward the end of one's life.

A person in late adulthood would seem to have an advantage with a Lost and Found Lover, who is no doubt also remembering the past: The sweethearts can reminisce about shared aspects of their youth that might even have been forgotten by one of them. A woman in her seventies expressed these thoughts:

WHEN I MET MY LOST Lover, I was fifteen and he was eighteen. We were real pals, went everywhere together, until I moved away. I married, but after forty-two years my husband died suddenly. I was alone six years when my brother told me that my Lost Lover's wife had also died.

Well, he called my mother—then ninety-one years old—and got

my phone number. He called and asked if he could come see me. I said, "Of course." He came and it was really wonderful. He stayed a week, and asked me to marry him. I sold my house in four days, and here I am married two years.

Now we are two of the happiest people. That old love is back again and we do everything together. My mom is ninety-three and thinks he's the greatest ever. We live on a lake in Idaho. Play a lot of bingo and reminisce a lot about our past.

Reviewing their memories helps people reorganize and reinterpret events, and it may even change their personalities for the better. When they finally sense what is truly important about living, they find it easier to accept mortality. Their losses—perhaps of health, home, possessions, career status, and income, or the death of friends and spouse—help them focus on what remains. One woman described a series of late life losses that served as catalysts for renewed romance:

WHEN I GRADUATED FROM HIGH school, in 1925, I asked a boy from a neighboring school if he would escort me to my prom. He did, and from then on we dated. That fall we both got jobs and saved our money, and the following year we enrolled at the same college. He dated other girls and I dated other boys. After college we went our separate ways.

He married one of my best friends. They were married less than two years when she was in an automobile accident that completely paralyzed her, and after many years she died from complications from her paralysis. He remarried a year later.

After that wife died, he moved to Boston to live with his daughter.

Meanwhile, jobs were scarce when I graduated, so I went on to graduate school for a master's degree. I married, but my husband died a few years later. My sister Rose, a teacher, moved in with me. After we both retired, we moved to Miami. We both developed macular degeneration and became legally blind. We had to depend more and more on our neighbors for help. Then Rose fell and broke her hip and had to be taken to a hospital, then a nursing home.

A few days later, I received a call from my Lost Lover. He had been talking to a mutual friend of ours in Boston, and she told him of my plight. As a result, he phoned to see how things were. I invited him to come visit me, and he accepted. He stayed a few days, then returned to Boston. A few days after his return, he called me again to ask how I was doing. I invited him to come back and see me. He answered, "If I do, will you marry me?" Of course I answered, "Yes!" He loaded up his car and headed south. We had a home wedding. Rose came home just for the day, then returned to the nursing home. His daughters were there, and a few old friends.

Arthur and I are very happily married, very much in love and trying our best to make up for all of those years. I am eighty-four and Arthur is eighty-six. Thank you.

Renewal

For most seniors, the most meaningful focus of their last years will be the family and friends they love. A woman in her eighties commented on this:

I CALLED MY LOST LOVER when I was in my late seventies to offer him some pictures of our early dating years and some pictures of him as a child. I got his address and sent him the pictures in a Christmas card. He called me as soon as he got back from his vacation.

We are happily married to each other now. Our romance is a little different in that this is a mature commitment, and the young love affairs seem to be "here today, and gone tomorrow," I think.

Most married, older people will eventually have to face the crises of their partner's illness, aging, and death. Not many of these surviving spouses marry again. One reason is that there are far more widows than widowers. And many older people believe that marrying someone else would be a betrayal of their deceased spouses. A lack of energy or money often keeps seniors from meeting new partners. All these reasons add up to the fact that many remarriages in this age group are between people who have previously known each other. One woman in her seventies wrote about her rekindled marriage:

WE MARRIED VERY YOUNG. OUR parents disapproved because we were from different religions and different ethnic groups. One New Year's Eve we met at his mother's house. That year was the thirty-ninth anniversary of our divorce! We resumed living together and a few months later we remarried. If our first marriage to each other had not ended, we would be married forty-nine years by now.

We both had been married to others in the interim: me for twenty-seven years before becoming a widow, and he for twenty-eight years before becoming a widower. Do we feel young again? You better believe it!

Is it possible to wait too long to reconnect? Unfortunately, it is. Over the years, the ill health of one or both Lost and Found Lovers might preclude their reunion. One widower in his late eighties proposed marriage, but it was not to be:

MY LOST LOVER AT EIGHTY-EIGHT years old is now blind. The friend who read my letters to her is no longer available so I don't write anymore, but I do phone her weekly. For the last year she has been in a nursing home, and I visited her there on her birthday.

This seems to be ending not with a bang but with a whimper. One of the personnel at the nursing home remarked that she seems full of anger and certainly nothing I say pleases her anymore. I realize that I'm dealing with a woman who is chronically ill, but since I can't seem to help her in any way and seem only to bother her, I wonder if it would not be best simply to end the relationship entirely.

P.S. During our original relationship, the song "Smoke Gets in Your Eyes" was popular and she was always humming it. When I went back to see her for her eighty-eighth birthday, I brought a recording of it. She did not seem to enjoy it! Our reunion seems to have come too late.

I suspect, from the letters I received from older women still looking for their Lost Lovers, that there would be even more rekindled romances at this stage if only the male Lost Lovers had survived. One man in his seventies who did live to rekindle an old friendship wrote to me to tell their story:

ABOUT TWO YEARS AFTER MY wife of fifty-one years passed away, I renewed acquaintance with a friend from early childhood. We had not seen each other for exactly forty-nine years and had remained in contact solely by Christmas cards.

When we met again, with some trepidation on both sides, we discovered so many low-probability coincidental parallels in our incredibly complex separate lives that it was uncanny.

She is a six-hour drive from me, but I visit her once a month. We have flown the Concorde to London and returned on the *Queen Elizabeth 2*. We are now planning several days in the wine country and a hot-air balloon ride. Finding things to do that we have not done with our spouses has taken some imagination!

A romance at our ages (over seventy) has had its difficulties, but we are overcoming them with a love as deep as either of us has ever known.

D URING THE TWO YEARS that I gathered data for the Lost Love Project, I collected and analyzed 1,001 questionnaires (see Appendix III for a copy of the questionnaire and a tabulation of the responses). After a first question about how many times they had renewed relationships, the next several questions asked about the initial romance. This chapter focuses on the Lost and Found Lovers' initial romances.

Most of the participants (82%) reconnected with only one Lost Lover, but some tried relationships with more than one. Most of these multi-rekindlers (13%) reconnected with two Lost Lovers, but a few met with three, four, or even more than four. One woman, approaching her fiftieth birthday, wrote to tell me that she had been contacted by six former boyfriends, all during that one year! Another woman in her fifties explained her reconnections:

> DURING TIMES OF TRANSITION, I have sought to contact Lost Lovers or friends from the past. This has been important in helping me "find myself" or put to rest questions about the past so that I could move on in my life.
>
> This has given me back a part of my solid identity from childhood which had been wounded or mislaid in my adult years. These renewed friendships have had a healing effect on others as well!

Some people rekindled a romance with one particular person more than once. A woman who renewed her romance three times with the same person wrote:

MY HUSBAND AND I HAVE known each other since we were fifteen years old. We double-dated in high school, he with another girl, I with another boy. When we started dating each other, my parents broke us up.

We went our separate ways. He got married and had a child. I married and made a mess of it. When I got divorced, we started seeing each other again (he was still married). Eventually we had a big fight and quit seeing each other. I started seeing another man and after a couple years got married. This marriage did not work out either and I got divorced again.

My Lost Lover called and asked me to have a drink after work. I accepted. We started seeing each other after he got a divorce and we lived together for about a year and then got married and have been married for sixteen years.

Another Lost Love Project participant wrote:

HE CONTACTED ME AS PART of "12 Step Amends" (this last time). We had previously tried to reestablish several times, but he kept changing the level of commitment. So we basically remained (romantically inclined) friends.

Just a few months after this call, we married. After eighteen years, we are still very happy, and have twins!

Occasionally, things do not work out no matter how many times one tries, as this man in his fifties learned:

I STILL LOVE MY LOST Lover but after five tries I will never allow myself to try again. In fact, after the fifth reunion, I finally remembered why we divorced in the first place.

Nevertheless, one couple is now married . . . on their sixth try together! Some of these persistent, optimistic lovers certainly follow the old adage "If at first you don't succeed, try, try again."

A PROFILE OF THE ORIGINAL RELATIONSHIPS

One of the most powerful reasons that drives people to try to reconnect is their memory of early love. More than half (55%) of the survey participants tried to rekindle a romance with someone they had loved when they were seventeen years old or younger. They had been young teenagers or even children, immersed in what many adults dismiss as "puppy love," yet these early love experiences were so meaningful that they drew the childhood sweethearts together again years later. Despite the passage of time, geographical distance, intervening romantic attachments, or other obstacles, people pursued these loves rather than more recent attachments from the past, and rather than searching for new loves.

Twenty-nine percent of the respondents reported that they had been eighteen to twenty-two years old during the initial romance—the traditional age of college students. When we add this percentage to the 55% that were seventeen or younger, we discover that 84% of the people in the Lost Love Project were younger than twenty-two when they first fell in love—still in what psychology textbooks consider the adolescent period.

Another 10% of the sample were twenty-three to twenty-nine when they first met the love with whom they later rekindled—still considered youths by social scientists. Few respondents were in their thirties (4%), and even fewer in their forties (2%) or older.

Considering the young age of the participants during the first romance, we would expect a large percentage of these Lost Lovers to have been first loves, and 62% of them reported that they were. But that leaves a sizable number of participants who rekindled with people who were not their first loves. It must be remembered, however, that the questionnaire gathered data from only one member of a rekindled couple. Perhaps the romance represented a first love for the other person, and that might have been the motivation for the renewed romance. This information is not known because this question was not asked (the survey was designed to avoid inaccurate guesses by one partner about the other).

The questionnaires revealed that the probability that a couple would remain together was significantly greater if the Lost Lover was the respondent's first love: 78% of all those respondents who checked "Yes" (this was a first love) also checked "We Are Still Together" later in the questionnaire. Only 66% of the respondents who reconnected with someone who was not their first love were still together. This difference was highly significant statistically (see Appendix III). Clearly, if the desired outcome of a rekindled romance is to remain together, people should look for that special someone who was their very first love.

In spite of the fact that 84% of the respondents had their initial relationships when they were twenty-two years old or younger, their original relationships were relatively long. Although 36% lasted a year or less, another 37% lasted from one to three years, and the remaining 27% continued even longer.

Because the people contributing to the Lost Love Project varied in age from teenagers to eighty-year-olds, it is not surprising that they reported considerable differences in the amount of sexual involvement and level of commitment in the initial romances. For example, 46% of them said that they dated without sexual involvement the first time around. Of course, many of the older people grew up in a time when sexual activity outside of marriage was much rarer than it is today. In some subcultures and parts of the United States, and in some other countries, it is still forbidden. It would be a mistake to conclude that these couples were not deeply involved or committed just because they were sexually abstinent. One man wrote about his sincere—and nonsexual—early love:

WE FIRST MET ONE ANOTHER at a bible school in Tennessee in 1942, both sophomores. My Lost Lover was a beautiful girl who radiated inner beauty through the most impressive eyes I had ever seen. I had been "hit by a freight train"—I fell instantly in love with her. I became determined to know her better.

It was for this reason that I saved a seat for her when the very first meal was served that year. Fortunately for me, she accepted. This was the beginning of us dining together regularly. We also had classes together, and I walked her to class, carrying her books. I always held her in high esteem and was so very proud to be seen with her. And she had a soft and loving disposition and the most beautiful smile I had ever seen.

Georgia had another trait that I had never known before: She had an ever-present aura of total and complete innocence shining through her pretty smile.

The following year my father took ill, and I had to leave school and get a full-time job to help with the family bills. Meanwhile Georgia continued her studies, finished early, and went off to college. When my father returned to work, I wanted desperately to be near her, so I moved near her college to look for a job. I tried for three months, but after that my funds were nonexistent, and I had to go home.

Then we were 500 miles apart. Phone calls were prohibitively expensive in those days, and not a very good substitute for personal contact in a romance anyway. Georgia was getting pressure from her parents and friends to date other boys, not wait around for one too poor to make the trip to see her. So eventually she gave in to the pressure and wrote me a "Dear John" letter. I was not surprised, but I was devastated and felt like my heart had been ripped out and beaten to a pulp. I wished her well and hoped someday she would change her mind.

Time marched on, and we each married others, even though the torch of love still burned in my heart for Georgia. Our marriages ended in divorce.

One day in 1987, I had a heart attack. While I was hospitalized, I went through the fear that my death was imminent, and I had an overwhelming need to find Georgia. I had not heard from her in all those years, but I had to tell her that I loved her from the very first sight of her, and that I never stopped loving her. Only then could I die in peace.

After many dead-end attempts to locate her, our old bible school agreed to forward a letter to her from me. To make a long story short, we discovered our long lost love once again, and married. I cannot imagine any man being happier than I am. She is, and always has been, the love of my life.

On the other hand, the fact that 48% of the respondents said they dated each other with sexual involvement does not necessarily mean that they felt a deep commitment, because they might have been dating—unlike the abstainers—in a time when sexual activity before marriage was more the norm and did not necessarily imply any commitment. But whether or not there was sexual involvement has very little to do with the emotional importance of a former sweetheart, or with the later drive to renew the romance.

Additionally, 7% of the participants said that they had lived together during the initial phase of their relationship; 10% had been engaged; and 6% had even been married the first time around. A woman now in her fifties shared this story:

MY LOST LOVER AND I came from different religions and social backgrounds. We married when we were both nineteen—two kids who had to bring each other up and didn't know how. We didn't know how to be committed, loving, and kind.

We have four children, and throughout our separation, they remained a thread which tied us together. We didn't divorce because we stopped loving one another, but because we were both very unhappy and after three years of marriage counseling, didn't see the situation changing for the better.

While we were separated, each of us married the first available person who came by. Of course, these second marriages didn't work. They both fell apart at about the same time. Both of us needed a place to stay, so we landed at our daughter's home.

We filed for divorce and married each other the day the divorces became final. It's been a year now, and we are very happy. Our regrets include 1) the hurt we caused our children, each other, and our ex-spouses, and 2) that we hadn't learned to be loving many years ago!

WHY THE INITIAL RELATIONSHIPS ENDED

Strong as the original relationships may have been, the forces working against them were even stronger. The reasons that couples break up are varied but universal. Many of them have repeated for centuries and will continue to plague lovers for centuries more.

Forty-five percent of the initial romances of the Lost Love Project were ended by the women. The men initiated 33% of the breakups. The remainder (23%) ended by mutual consent. Other surveys have consistently found an even higher percentage (66%) of women who end romances—contrary to the popular stereotype that men are usually the heartbreakers.

Despite the young age of most of the participants during the initial romance, only a few (11%) reported that age was the primary reason for the breakup. One woman in Canada who did believe that youth had worked against her wrote:

> I MET A MAN I loved and I believed he loved me. Spiritually it felt right. But he had been twice married, and I didn't know if this was real love to him (it was to me) or if I was just the next in a procession. I became pregnant right away. We were very poor. He was a struggling musician and I was a waitress.
>
> After our child was born, we were getting into debt. I took a job as a live-in nanny. I wanted him to take a stand and say "no," but he didn't. Within three months, he was living with another woman, had a real job, and even bought her an engagement ring. I was shattered. I lost a lot of weight and suffered a nervous breakdown, I believe. Then I moved back to my home province. There I became

a Christian, gradually feeling better about myself, putting the past behind me, working, and building a life for my daughter and me.

We kept in touch now and then. He phoned when my dad died. When our daughter was eight, he came back again and moved in with us. We were married when she was nine, and I was pregnant with our second daughter.

It's been a rough road but our love was real. And that's what I always believed—you go with love. Now I know other things are important besides love. Like planning for the future together, and friendship, companionship, sharing the same faith. We were just too young before.

Many (23%) young loves ended because of physical separation. People moved away or went away to school. Foreign exchange students had to return to their countries and leave their sweethearts behind. One man wrote about his many relocations:

WE ARE BOTH ORIGINALLY FROM California. Later, I moved to Ohio to live with her. Then she went to Mexico on a trip, fell in love, got married, and eventually moved to Europe. Eight years later, I was traveling in Japan and I heard that she and her husband were two or three days ahead of me. The next summer in India we ran into each other, and several years later in Sweden we had an affair. Then I returned to the United States. After her marriage broke up, I flew to Europe to spend some time with her.

Four or five years later, she returned to California and we tried to live together. Although we still loved each other, she had a health problem that made it impossible for me. She is still in the area, and I hear about her occasionally.

Considering the young ages of many of these sweethearts when they embarked on their romance the first time, one might expect many breakups to be caused by friction about commitment. But only 9% broke up because one partner wanted a commitment that the other could not make.

A larger percentage (13%) of the initial romances ended because one of the partners began dating someone else. This situation might be a more serious breach of the romance than different attitudes toward commitment, because the dating might have been covert and thus a betrayal of trust. One man wrote of the devastation he experienced during the initial romance after he discovered the unfaithfulness of his partner:

> THERE WAS BETRAYAL, YES. BUT even worse was the destruction of reality as I knew it. My memories of us as the Happy Couple were suddenly proven false. So what *was* real about our past together? I didn't know anymore.

Sometimes the tables are turned and the choice to remain with a committed love—the respondent or the lover could not leave a marriage or significant other—ended the initial romance. However, only 49 couples (5%) cited this reason as the deciding factor in their breakup.

Surprisingly few couples said that they initially broke up because they were not getting along (3%) or had no common interests (6 people). Not one of the first loves cited these as their reasons for breaking up. These reasons reflect personal characteristics—the "fit" of people's personalities, and their values, hobbies, and way of life.

This fact may explain why rekindled relationships have such a good chance of success. The rekindlers did not choose to go back to incompatible lovers. The main reasons cited for the initial breakups were situational, not psychological—reasons that may be long gone when rekindlers meet again five or more years later.

About 7% of the couples broke up initially because they had different expectations. This might indicate communication problems. One partner might have assumed that the relationship was headed in a certain direction, while the other partner had other ideas. Perhaps the lovers were inept at sharing their feelings, or maybe one partner purposely concealed information from the other. One of the lovers might have denied the differences, despite the evidence, or tried to change the sweetheart over time. When these couples finally realized how seriously they disagreed about the meaning of the romance, they could see no alternative to breaking up.

Differences in expectations might very well doom a couple's later attempts to try to rekindle their romance. Although people often become better communicators as they mature, this is not always the case. One woman who did manage eventually to fulfill her expectations shared her story:

I WAS THIRTY-FIVE AND HAD never been married. I was always fighting a weight problem. But I had recently lost sixty pounds and my social life was taking off. My girlfriend and I decided to move to Los Angeles from Texas to look for jobs. We got jobs as bank tellers in a nice neighborhood. We were having a drink after work one evening when Ed sat beside me—an event that changed my life forever. The attraction for both of us was immediate.

For the next year, I chased Ed with the vision of a wedding ring. I had grown up in an era when women were considered old maids if they were not married by their late twenties. I was in my "marriage or die" mode. However, he did not have the same goal. He had two ex-wives already and girlfriends all over town. The last thing on his mind was settling down.

After it became evident that Ed would not make a commitment to me, I left Los Angeles and returned to Texas, one year after I left it. Ed and I corresponded for a time, but eventually we lost contact. I thought about him many times, and cried myself to sleep. He had become the love of my life.

Eventually time healed my broken heart and I realized my dream of becoming a bride. Unfortunately, it turned out to be a seven-year nightmare. I went through a very stressful divorce, car accidents, job losses, and the death of my sister. With the support of my loving family, I began to heal from the traumas, and I then felt a very strong pull to return to California. My girlfriend and I went for a visit.

I found Ed easily through his union. He was unattached. His union rep told him there was a "little Southern magnolia" looking for him. He knew it was me. He was glad to see me but hesitant, still in his party mode. I decided to take a chance and move there. Using my friend's idea, I asked Ed if I could stay with him a few days until I found a place to live. However, a few days after my move, he lost his job. He had no savings, and it hit him hard. We decided to stick together, and I became the guest who never left. Two years later I got my wish: Ed asked me to marry him on the fifteenth anniversary of our first meeting. We were married on the beach, surrounded by friends.

The Lost Love Project questionnaire included the category "Other" for people to check to explain why their initial romances ended. Of course such a category is very broad, but the responses (8%) almost always fell into three subcategories.

The most common explanation was that the man enlisted or was drafted into the military, or was otherwise separated from his Lost Lover because of a war. Harry L. Bioletti, author of *The Yanks Are Coming,* told me that during World War II, hundreds of young women in New Zealand had dated American servicemen who had been stationed there from 1942 to 1944. Sometimes the men returned after a few years to renew their romances, but in many other cases, the lovers were reunited only fifty years later, when the men returned for fifty-year reunions of their military units. Several of these American–New Zealand romances are represented in the Lost Love Project.

A woman from Massachusetts wrote about a different reason for a Lost Love separation caused by World War II:

I HAVE COME FULL CIRCLE. The friend of my youth has come back into my life, and over fifty years have fallen away. It seems like only yesterday that we parted in Berlin. We can still recall the plays and operas and movies that we saw together, and our subway rides each morning to go to school.

He remembers that I slapped his face when he tried to kiss me, but I suppose I have conveniently forgotten that. At sixteen I wasn't ready for that kind of intimacy. After all, it was 1936. How young and innocent we were!

Our joy ended when he left Germany for France, where he survived the Holocaust by living with French relatives, and with false papers. He wrote until he lost track of me, when my family left for the United States, where we were so much safer than our loved ones caught in Europe. Soon after I arrived here, the war started, France was occupied, and all communication ended.

After he found me again, he lost no time writing and calling. We talked almost daily, catching up on the lost years. He had never married. I asked him to visit me, and he booked a flight. But I was stunned when he said he expected to stay three weeks. I asked myself if we could really recapture feelings we had experienced as adolescents. After all, we had been so young and had been together such a short time. And our lives had been so different—what if we couldn't stand each other? He told me later that he had had similar thoughts.

I guess miracles can still happen. We need not have worried. The minute we met at the airport and embraced, all doubts disappeared. We took up where we left off—new movies, plays, classical music, and sight-seeing. He brought a tape of the hit songs we used to like from the thirties. We felt young again. And this time I let him kiss me.

Nothing can replace a common background, shared experiences, and memories. I can hardly believe that, at our age, we have been given a new chapter in our lives. My daughter, at first skeptical of our reconnection, now says, "Mother, you deserve it!" Although I don't think "deserving" has any bearing on one's fate, those words from my daughter were greatly appreciated.

A second explanation that commonly appeared in the "Other" category was that the young woman became pregnant. The fears about the pregnancy, or feelings about adoption or abortion, created an insurmountable barrier, as this woman in her thirties wrote:

OUR RELATIONSHIP ENDED AFTER ALMOST two years of
dating because I had become pregnant. I was so scared! I was eighteen, and he was twenty, and we were so in love. But he wasn't
ready to have a family (neither was I). When I went to his house
to talk to him, he got scared. So he told me he didn't love me
anymore. I told him I wouldn't have the child, and I cried and
pleaded with him not to break up with me. He did, though, and it
broke my heart.

I couldn't tell my parents, so I told my best friend's mom, and
they helped me get an abortion. After almost a year, I started dating
someone else.

When my best friend got married, I was a bridesmaid and he
was an usher. We left the rehearsal at about the same time. He drove
up beside my car with tears streaming down his face, whispering, "I
love you." But my pride was hurt along with my feelings. But I never
hated him. I felt like a lost soul for months after that, and I carried
a lot of pain. Still do in certain aspects.

After ten years we reunited. We have been together now for five
years, and we are married. We are both very happy. We have talked
about the past and what happened. I think the hardest part for me
is that I had the chance then to have his child, but I can't now because
of a hysterectomy. But we do, thank goodness, have children from
our prior marriages, and we both love them very much.

"Other" often included initial romances in which one or both of the lovers
were addicted to alcohol or other drugs. A woman wrote from South Carolina
to share her journey back to sobriety and renewed romance:

FRANK AND I MET WHEN we were in kindergarten, and fell in
love in high school. The chemistry was certainly there. But his family
convinced him that I was not good for him. He left me on New
Year's Eve, and I will never forget the hurt.

In 1989, due to a traumatic family incident, I got sober. It took
time for me to rebuild my life, but I grew and learned to really love

myself and others. I kept thinking about Frank, and went to the school reunion, but he wasn't there. I did learn that he was divorced and uninvolved. I wrote him a letter, and he called a few days later. I moved to South Carolina to be with him the following New Year's Day. We are engaged and as happy as a couple of kids. He, too, is now clean and sober in Alcoholics Anonymous.

We believe that God wanted to save the best for last for us, and that's why it took so long for us to be together. My heart overflows with joy whenever I read about other couples who have renewed their romances. One day at a time, we live the magic.

A few reasons were more unusual. Two couples said that they were each other's first cousins, and fears about bearing developmentally disabled offspring caused them to separate. A U.S. Air Force officer lost his address book when his plane was shot down during World War II and he became a prisoner of war in Stalag Luft III for almost two years. One man left the initial romance to become a priest. And another man was left behind when his sweetheart became a cloistered nun:

IN 1943 I FELL IN love with a beautiful young lady but I was helpless to do anything about it. She was committed to go into a cloistered convent and I was still a student. After an idyllic summer, we parted, never to see one another until last year.

In the intervening years, my Lost Lover fulfilled her commitment to God and spent thirty years in the convent. She left and married a man who had left the priesthood. He must have been a wonderful man, because he is well remembered and he was loved. He succumbed to an illness, and my Lost Lover was saddened. But she set out to make a life for herself, and when I rediscovered her, she was totally content.

I had been separated for ten years. So Jesus brought her back into my life, and did so after my Lost Lover had mourned and was ready for a new beginning. I had fulfilled all my obligations, too, and now I have someone to love and care for, and to share my future.

Parental disapproval was by far the number-one reason (25%) that couples separated the first time, especially the first loves. These teenagers listened to their parents, even to the point of ending a romance that was very important to them. They did not rebel. They did not do much sneaking behind the parents' backs (although some respondents admitted to doing this before they broke up). They cried, and then complied. One woman described this type of ending, and the parental situation that brought them back together later:

MY LOST LOVER AND I were engaged when we were in college in the early forties. But my parents would not allow it, and those were the days when you did as your parents told you. They went so far as to en-roll me in another college a great distance away from him. My parents felt I would not be happy with a farm boy. We tried to elope a few times but were never successful, and we eventually gave up.

I had a very happy marriage for twenty-seven years, and never expected to see my Lost Lover again. Andy later told me that he kept up with me through the college alumni magazine.

To make a very long story short, my husband died. And Andy's wife was abusive, so he eventually divorced. He was living in Florida by then. He wrote to me and asked me to check up on the health of his mother. I did, and wrote to him that I thought she needed his immediate attention, that he'd better come see for himself.

I picked him up at the airport to drive him to his mother's house. He was balding but I would have known him anywhere. And it was just as if we had never been apart. We were married within a year, after thirty-two years apart. Evidently the spark never dimmed.

We have recently celebrated our twenty-fifth anniversary, but it seems just like yesterday that we got married. We live in heavenly Georgia. I don't know how we were so lucky but it was worth the wait. I adore that man. He is kind, thoughtful, giving, supportive of me and my children, and sexy still!!!

The strange part is that I thought I had a great husband the first time. Little did I know! Someone said it is better the second time around. That depends on if the second time around is to the love you lost many years before.

A substantial number (11%) of Lost Love Project participants reported that their parents broke apart their romances because their sweethearts were from different races or ethnic groups, different religions, different socioeconomic groups, or because of a big age gap between them, as was the case for this Michigan couple:

I AM MARRIED TO MY childhood sweetheart. We will celebrate our twenty-fifth wedding anniversary next spring. We originally went together for over three years and got engaged. But parents broke us apart: When we started dating I was only thirteen and he was eighteen. We were apart for seven years.

The day I heard he was getting married, I locked myself in the bathroom and cried for two hours.

We got back together, and married, after our divorces. Between us, we have six wonderful children (his two, my one, and our three) and five grandchildren so far!

Another group reported that they defied their parents and dated anyway; ultimately these relationships ended for reasons other than parental interference. One woman tells of her experience fifty years ago:

WE MET ON A BLIND date set up by a mutual friend. We doubled with them for dinner. It was a whirlwind romance, and he was the love of my life. Circumstances, however, were not in our favor. For starters, he was Jewish and I was Catholic. We lived in two different cities. And he was also in the Navy (it was World War II).

He was sent off to the Philippines. I waited. We resumed dating after the war but again we lived far apart and lost touch. Time went by and I married and started a business. He married and also owned a business. He was widowed. About two years ago, the same old friend put us back in touch with each other.

I picked him up at the train station and we returned to the restaurant where we met on our first date. When we danced, all the feelings came back. Within the week, we decided to marry. It just happened. I'm using the original friendship ring he gave me as our wedding band. It seems only appropriate.

Before the civil rights movement of the sixties, some teenagers did not want to date across racial, ethnic, or religious lines. It was also more difficult back then to meet and date people of wide socioeconomic or age differences, because adolescents were limited to neighborhood schools, church or synagogue youth groups, and family sanctioned clubs. Also, parents did most of the driving, at least in the suburbs and rural areas.

Today, teens routinely attend schools outside their neighborhoods to take advantage of magnet programs featuring educational specialties or in "open enrollment" school districts. These educational innovations began as ways to bring together teens of different racial and ethnic backgrounds. Furthermore, roughly half of adolescents today work during high school, and they often have their own cars. This wider exposure to the outside world and greater freedom from parents makes daily contact with people of diverse backgrounds more common, leading teens to date teens of different backgrounds more often today than they did back when most of the Lost Love Project participants began their romances.

The respondents who chose to "date out" of their own group and then broke off their romances because of parental disapproval represent a middle approach. That is, they risked their parents' disapproval by dating someone "different," but when parental push came to shove, they complied and broke off the relationships.

Another common explanation (6%) for parental interference was that one or more of the couple's parents simply said they did not like the sweetheart. Of course, there might have been other factors, such as the "differences" discussed above, that the parents chose not to talk about. And maybe no one would have been "good enough" for their son or daughter back then. One woman, now in her fifties and happily married to her Lost and Found Lover, told a story illustrating the extreme measures some parents took to separate their child from the first love:

> MY LOST LOVER AND I dated for the last two years of high school. My mother and father forced us apart. They just didn't like him. They never said why. After they separated us, we ran away together. We were caught, and felony charges were pressed against him. So the law stepped in and forced us apart even further. My parents moved me away and I had no idea he was looking for me.
>
> I continued to search, even through two marriages, on and off for thirty years, and he did as well. I finally found one of his relatives through Directory Assistance and got his phone number. We were married six months later, and we have a wonderful life now. *Hooray!!*
>
> We both had thirty years of unnecessary pain. I think if we could have been left alone then, we would have stayed together.

Other couples broke up because their parents thought they were too young (6%). As discussed earlier, another 11% said that they broke up because they considered themselves to be too young the first time. So youthfulness is an important reason why the initial romances end, even though parents and their adolescents may not agree about who is too young. One woman, now in her forties and living with her Lost Lover, recounted her experience:

> MY LOST LOVER WAS A blind date for my junior prom. He joined the Navy and was sent to Japan. My father was in the Navy and was also sent to Japan. It was not until I arrived there that I found out Bob's ship was stationed at the same base. We had a little

over a year there together, and during that time we got engaged.

My father thought we were too young, so he sent me back to the USA. Since we did not have addresses to write to each other, we lost each other.

After we found each other and talked about it, I found out that he had been looking for me and had gone to my father to ask where I was. My father would not tell him. I was really upset about that!

My father died many years ago—before I reunited with Bob— so I was not able to talk to him about it and tell him how hurt I was over it. Thinking about the "lost years" really ate at me. I wish my Lost and Found Lover had been the father of the three children I did have. I often wonder what might have been.

Only a few people (3%) reported that their parents had broken up their romances out of fear of their sexual involvement. This percentage seems low, but how often would parents, even today, be willing to voice this fear unless they had some concrete proof of sexual activity? And even if they had such knowledge, how often would they risk discussing it? Although parents might be able to muddle through a conversation about safe sex or other general sexual topics, most parents find it almost impossible to talk frankly and specifically about the sexuality of their adolescents.

Parents who fear that an adolescent couple is too intimate might find it much easier to suggest other reasons why the couple should spend less time together. Accordingly, parents who said they thought the lovers were too young might really have been worried about their teenagers' sexual activities.

Parents who did not like the lover's personality might have had similar concerns (as in, "This guy seems likely to take advantage of my innocent young daughter," or, "This girl seems likely to get my innocent young son in trouble"). One man in his forties described how he felt:

WE WERE THIRTEEN WHEN WE met. I was someone "bad" to her entire family, because we were *believed* to be sexually active then (but we weren't). To this day, that old stigma weighs on her family's memory. When I am around her mom and sisters, I still feel thirteen sometimes.

Would some of these parents "come clean" about their concerns if their adult children discussed the romance with them now? I don't know. But I did receive some letters that indicated these grown children had a few things to say to parents:

I MET MY LOST LOVER when I was in the ninth grade. It was not the healthiest relationship in hindsight, but we both desperately needed someone to love and accept us. I was the youngest in a very strict minister's family. I became pregnant with my Lost Lover's child when I was eighteen. I didn't know then that he offered to marry me. My parents only gave me two options: abortion, or a baby raised forever to be my sister. I chose abortion.

They drove me to another state where abortion was legal. My parents went sight-seeing while I aborted a ten-week-old fetus. Then my parents forbade me to see my Lost Lover again. This will forever haunt me, and was the reason, in counseling, that I contacted my Lost Lover in later years.

If I could offer one word of advice to parents who do not approve of the person their son or daughter is dating, it would be to just let time take its course. The parents' angry disapproval has a boomerang effect, and if not resolved it will come back to haunt later in life, hurting many more people. That love has always continued to be a part of me every day!

A social worker in New York also wished to offer her story—and a message to parents of teenagers:

MY HUSBAND AND I FIRST met when we were young teenagers. We went together for three years before my parents broke us up. First, unbeknownst to me, they were not mailing my letters and gifts to him after he left for California with the Air Force. He knew something was wrong, so he mailed an engagement ring to get my attention.

My parents cursed and screamed at me to give back the ring. They threatened to have him arrested for "corrupting the morals of a minor." My father (a police officer) told me it was a felony and that Rich would go to jail for the rest of his life. It broke my heart to think of Rich in jail, so I signed the "Dear John" letter that my father dictated to me the next day.

My grades fell, and I started drinking. I didn't care about anything, and after a while I couldn't feel anything.

Our lives were shattered: I married anyone just to get away from home, and my Lost Lover did the same. I spent many years in therapy because of this situation. What my parents did was so extreme and so devastating, it is hard even for me to believe.

I hope that, through your research, parents will learn that their adolescents *do* often know best about whom they should love, and who are the best partners for them. Our children deserve our love and understanding and support of their feelings, not abuse. I do not advocate teen marriages, but I think parents should permit the loves if marriage is postponed until after school is completed.

We reunited after thirty-five years. When I miraculously found my Lost Lover, now my husband, we both felt as if the world had turned right-side-up, and everything was the way it was supposed to be. We both feel that nothing, not even death, could separate us again.

Although 9% of the Lost Lovers reported that they recovered quickly (in less than one month) after their initial separation, most were not so lucky. It took up to a year for 39% of them to regain their emotional balance. Another 21% said that it took up to three years; for 13% it took as long as ten years. And a full 17%—all first loves—said that it took more than ten years to recover emotionally from the loss of this loved one—which meant, as many people noted (all of them men), that they never recovered at all!

So the next time parents or friends are tempted to make light of a broken romance by calling it "puppy love," or by trying to comfort a grieving Lost Lover by saying that "a romance is like a bus . . . a new one comes along every ten minutes," or by mailing the Lost Lover a newspaper page with circled singles ads, perhaps they will think twice. Some romances are irreplaceable, and—as Nat "King" Cole tells us in the well-known song—some lovers are unforgettable. Some losses must be grieved over for a long, long time, until maybe, one day, the two will meet as sweethearts once again.

*I*N THIS CHAPTER, WE will see how the Lost Love Project participants found each other again, how these rekindled romances differ from other types of love, potential land mines to avoid in seeking out a Lost Lover, and the rewards of successfully rekindling a Lost and Found Love.

HOW THEY FOUND EACH OTHER

If the ending of the original romance was not mutually agreed upon, I wondered which of the Lost Lovers was most likely to make the first move toward reconnecting. One might think the person who left would feel sorry for his or her actions long ago and would want to reconnect to explain, to apologize, or to correct the errors of the past. But this scenario fit only 12% of the Lost and Found Loves. A larger percentage (23%) reported that their attempts to rekindle were mutual.

Sixty-three percent of these couples came together again because of the lover who was originally left—the "dumpee." Did this partner, presumably hurt the first time, walk around for years thinking, "Someday I'll show him/her!" Did this person want to collect a debt—heal a bruised ego, or finally right the wrong? Did these Lost and Found Lovers just want to ask the question that always hovered in the back of their minds: "Why did you leave me?" The answer is often "none of the above." People wrote that they just never got over the loss of that sweetheart and wanted another chance at that special love.

Where did they find each other again? Most likely not at the school reunion. The class reunion is very commonly cited in newspaper and television stories as the primary way that Lost Lovers reconnect. But only 6% of Lost Love Project couples began their rekindled romances this way. One reunion example came from a woman in her sixties:

MY LOST LOVER AND I dated all through our junior and senior years of high school and into our first year of college when, as he bluntly and accurately describes it, I dumped him for a fraternity guy. We each married and had children, and I divorced. We had no contact whatsoever until our twenty-fifth high school reunion. He was the first person I saw when I entered the room. As I chatted with classmates, the MC asked if we remembered what we had said was our favorite song in the school newspaper twenty-five years earlier. I had no idea, but my Lost Lover blurted it out from across the room. I doubt if his wife got it, but I did. I knew there was still a very strong attraction between us.

Later we talked, and I was surprised at how much he knew about my present circumstances. As we talked our arms touched—very slightly—and neither of us moved. It was imperceptible to anyone else, but an intimate contact nonetheless.

After that he called me very occasionally, and we saw each other briefly at the thirtieth and thirty-fifth reunions. When my mother died, he called me to express condolences. From then on he called me monthly. He even took me out to dinner for my birthday, wearing the socks I'd knitted for him thirty-eight years before! It was a very strange sensation to know him—yet not to know him—all at once. Thirty-eight years just vanished.

Although he continued to call, it was another year before I saw him again, on my birthday. He told me he had separated from his wife. That was all I needed for a go-ahead.

I can't give a name to our relationship—it just is. It's both young and mature at the same time. The connection grows stronger and more intense each time we are together. It's the most intimate, passionate, and secure relationship of my life. It's lasted in various forms for over forty years—it isn't going to end now.

I've often wondered if it would have been this good if we'd just stayed together all those years ago. Maybe not. I might have taken him for granted and not appreciated the kind of man that he is.

Most of the participants in the Lost Love Project were risk takers. They did not wait passively until a reunion year came along. When one decided that it would be nice to see or hear from the Lost Lover again, he or she often wrote a letter. More than one fifth of the participants reconnected in this way. Another fifth found each other again through a friend or relative who brought the two together (by arranging a visit, a letter, or a telephone call), as one woman recounted:

I RECONNECTED WITH MY FIRST love after being apart for fifty-five years. We met when we were nineteen years old, at a junior college, and went steady for more than a year.

Then World War II was about to start and Pearl Harbor was imminent. Our lives drifted apart. I finished school and married a fine young man. We were married for forty-eight years. My husband died from cancer a couple of years ago.

My daughter saw how lonely I was and encouraged me to call anyone I could think of in my old hometown. Another daughter looked in a phone directory and found Jack, whom I had mentioned occasionally in the years of their growing up.

They pushed me to contact him and I did, and he remembered me and said he had been single for twenty-two years. He invited me to lunch and came to my home where we were reunited. We are both seventy-five years old now. We had a wonderful reunion and I felt that old spark rekindle, even though it had been over half a century since we last saw one another.

Even more (39%) of the participants simply picked up the telephone:

MY STORY BEGAN IN JULY, 1994, although you could also say
it started in 1965. One July night I hopped out of bed, where I was
comfortably reading, to answer the telephone. I grabbed a pencil on
the way to take down the inevitable message for one of my teenagers,
who were both out.

My "Hello" was followed by an unfamiliar, but very friendly and
appealing male voice asking for me by my maiden name, which only
a few people would know. Who was this? I couldn't figure.

"This is a telephone survey," he said. "If you can answer three
questions, you will receive a prize."

I asked who was calling several times, but he refused to tell me
until the end of the survey. "Okay!" I finally yelled into the phone.

"Okay, first question: Where is your favorite place to eat lunch?"

"I don't know. Who is this?!"

"Is that the name of the restaurant: I Don't Know?"

"Okay!" I gave him the name of a restaurant.

"Second question: Would you go out with someone you went out
with twenty-nine years ago?"

Then I knew who he was, but I didn't let on. "Sure," I said.

"You would? But you don't even know who this is."

"Well, I have such good taste in men, that if I went out with
them before, I would go out with them again."

There was much laughter from the other end of the phone. "Hi,
Janet. This is Eddie. How are you?"

"Hi, Eddie, I'm fine. How are you?"

And we've been together ever since.

In most cases, it was easy to find the Lost Lover—through old addresses
former employers, mutual friends, relatives who remained in the old hometown
school or military records, or professional associations or unions. One woman
wrote:

MY LOST LOVER AND I separated when we were twenty. It was a conversation in which I asserted that I was a career girl and didn't see myself marrying (read "scared of commitment"). He was furious at me and left. I called later when I realized my incredible sense of loss, but he hung up on me. That was the last I heard from him for thirty-five years.

I often thought of him. My fantasy was that we could have a long conversation in which we parted, healed. He said that he looked for me, too, to heal a wrong he had inflicted.

He eventually found me through my alumni association. His initial letter was very tentative. My reply was also tentative but we began a correspondence. He visited once and we were both very constrained and distant. But when he visited again, I fell in love with him in one of those moments in which it seems a window swings open. It was nothing that involved effort on his part, just a comfortable connection of empathy and humor.

Will schools or businesses give out direct information about Lost Lovers? No. But they will usually forward a letter, leaving it up to the recipient to decide whether to answer. Only a few respondents reported that it took great time and expense for them to find that sweetheart.

Only 10% of the respondents bumped into each other by chance. Another 2% of the couples reconnected after some mention of the Lost Lover in a newspaper article, or personal ad:

WE MET AND FELL IN love in 1973 on a kibbutz in Israel, when we were both volunteers during the Yom Kippur War. After about nine months, we both returned to the United States to finish school, and life just went on. We wrote for awhile, but in 1978 he got married, and then I got married, and at that point I decided it would be inappropriate to keep writing. We then lost contact for twelve years.

He knew I had been living in Israel when I was engaged. In 1989 he came to Israel after his divorce, to start over. He began looking for me, but he didn't know my married name. The next year he put an ad in the personals column of *The Jerusalem Post:* "Jackie, call Alan (Kibbutz Ein Gev, 1973) phone # . . ." I never read the personal ads, but a friend of mine who does saw it and asked if I could be the same Jackie. Of course I called him (I was divorced by then) and he came to visit. The attraction was very powerful and we've been together ever since. We are married.

We both feel we were too young and "unfinished" for it to have worked the first time, but we are *solid* this time! Our early shared experiences really do provide a sort of anchor, making us different from a couple who came together for the first time in their thirties. We feel very blessed to have found one another again.

One man wrote to describe a humorous reconnection through a newspaper story:

MY OLD LOVE CALLED ME out of the blue after disappearing from my life sixteen years before. She was divorced, and a relative sent her a newspaper article about my winning the Great Texas Barbecue Sauce Search. Now we are in the process of getting to know each other again.

We believe that this was destined to happen, and couldn't be happier about it. By the way, when she left me, I got into the blues and became a blues guitar player over the years. It was my way of dealing with the loss. Now I have to find a way to play the blues without actually living them!

Others heard about the former sweetheart on the radio or on television, mostly in news stories, but a few were purposely reunited on the air during a talk show. Some met again accidentally in a computer newsgroup, bulletin board, or on-line forum, and some used the various member directories to search for their Lost Lovers. One professor shared this story of his reconnection with his Lost Lover, now his wife:

DURING THE FIRST CALL, ONE of the many things I asked her was, "How did you know where I was?" She told me her husband, since deceased, had brought home one of my journal articles about ten years earlier, and she was able to update my university affiliation and address from there. I'd say this certainly gives a new twist to publish or perish.

The numbers are clear: Rekindlers are by and large assertive. Most purposefully pursued a chance for a second romance with their Lost Lovers by contacting them. Chance meetings at reunions or by walking along a crowded street were not for most of them. They willingly risked the Lost and Found Lovers' lack of interest, or a second heartbreak in a renewed relationship. One man offered some practical advice after visiting his long lost sweetheart's home during a reunion trip to New York:

IF YOU EVER THINK OF looking up your old girlfriend or boyfriend, don't surprise them. Give notice. They appreciate that. Trust me.

Another commonly held belief is that most couples wait twenty-five years or more to reunite. But a third of the respondents in this study reconnected within five to ten years. Another 17% waited from ten to fifteen years. Twelve percent waited from sixteen to twenty years, and another 11% from twenty-one to twenty-five years. And 10% of the couples in the Lost Love Project waited twenty-six to thirty years to renew their love.

The rekindled romances that take place after thirty years have passed are less common. Only 6% rekindled at the thirty-one-to-thirty-five-year point, but the percentage rises to 10% for people who renewed their love after thirty-six to forty years. Three people proudly claimed a forty-to-fifty-year absence from their Lost Lovers. Four couples had to wait more than fifty years, and one couple reunited after being apart for more than sixty years! But the waits are worth it. As one woman in her seventies wrote:

IT SEEMS IMPOSSIBLE THAT WE have now been married four-teen years. It seems like only yesterday we picked up where we left off forty-two years earlier. I had not planned or expected to fall for him again, but when he arrived in Boston from San Francisco and I picked him up at the airport, it was as if we had never been apart.

I thought I'd had a happy life with my husband and three price-less children, but until he and I married, I didn't know what happi-ness was.

These older couples are the ones most often celebrated in newspaper stories, and each truly deserves our applause. They are retired, or still working, or maybe volunteering in their communities. They might be widowed, or even newly di-vorced. Many have grown children, and some have grandchildren. Some are very ill, some suffer from aches and pains, others are still robust. But they are still romantic and optimistic, still risk takers, sexually active, and in need of adult love relationships. They write to me with lavender ink on flowered stationery, or from the SeniorNet to my e-mail address. Or they telephone me. In the winter of life, they have turned to the lovers of their springtime. Their road to reunion was long and winding, often hard to travel, but worth it. They report that they have never been happier. A woman now in her eighties wrote:

WE WERE APART FOR FIFTY-EIGHT years. We were both sev-enty-seven years old when all this happened. We were married in three months. We are very happy with each other—contented—and life has become complete.

A man separated from his Lost Lover for fifty-nine years shared this reunion account:

AT THE TIME OF OUR reconnection, we had both been widowed for almost four years. One day she read in our alumni newsletter about my retirement, and she wrote to the school for my address. Then she wrote to me. I was really excited.

We soon found that writing letters and waiting for an answer took too long, so we began talking on the phone. I was eighty-three and she was eighty-two.

I told her we were now living on borrowed time and we should make the most of every day. So I sent her a senior citizen's airline coupon book and asked her to come and visit me for a month. After much thought, she agreed, provided I would visit her in the same way. I agreed and we spent August together.

We both fell in love almost at once, and on her second visit to my home that November we were married. My family loves her. We hope we can keep our good health and have several happy years together.

The number of years a couple spent apart influences their chances for staying together the second time. Even though 34% of the Lost Love Project couples reconnected after only five to ten years, their rekindled romances had often ended by the time they filled out the questionnaire. Those who checked "We Are Still Together" were typically apart much longer (twenty-one years or more). Couples who had been parted the longest had the highest chances of remaining together in the rekindled romance. This difference was highly significant statistically.

HOW REKINDLED ROMANCES DIFFER FROM OTHERS

The geography of the rekindled couple is generally more complicated than in a typical new romance. When Lost Lovers find each other again, they sometimes discover that there are states or even whole continents between them.

One fourth of the Lost Love Project couples lived fewer than fifty miles apart (often without knowing it) when they renewed their love. But 36% were separated by more than 1,000 miles. For example, one man in Ireland wrote:

FOR THE LAST THREE YEARS, mainly on my initiative, we have been trying to find out what it is that triggers such strong responses between us, both positive and negative. We have tried breaking contact for months at a time, and since we live 5,000 miles apart, such occasions do seem like the end. However, it always starts up again.

I have tried to convince myself that she is just a fixation and to leave it alone, but we have seen each other despite the distance, and every time we do, she admits to strong feelings and a sense that we still have much to learn from each other. This is unlike any relationship I have ever had, including my marriage, and continues with such intensity that I can't help believing that the rediscovery of the Lost Love proper has yet to happen.

It is not surprising, then, that 32% of the participants reported spending an excessive amount of money on visits and activities, and 50% reported traveling frequently to be together.

Telephone charges can be high in these long distance relationships. Most of the Lost Love Project participants (61%) reported that they spent an excessive amount of time on the telephone, and their phone bills frequently ran to hundreds of dollars per month. One woman was philosophical about this expense: It pleased her that she accumulated airline miles with every dollar she spent on the telephone.

To cut down on these costs, 46% of these Lost and Found Lovers spent a lot of time writing letters. Some people (especially the first loves) found this method of communication too slow, however. They felt they had already lost too much time being apart. A compromise between the speedy but expensive telephone and "snail mail" was found by using overnight mail services or computer e-mail.

Surprisingly, the couples who were still together at the time of the survey had lived significantly farther apart when they began their rekindled romances than couples who parted again. Rekindlers who reported that they spent time thinking obsessively about the Lost and Found Lover, talking on the telephone, and writing letters also were statistically more likely to remain together. And almost every couple who used overnight delivery services or e-mail stayed together, as in this example of an extramarital affair:

LAST YEAR, MY JOB TOOK me away from home a lot for an extended project. Talking with her on the phone almost nightly was not a problem during this time. In fact, we were able to do this for five months, with breaks on the weekends when I went back home.

In addition to all the items listed on the questionnaire, we also sent each other "mushy" cards, and because of the required secrecy of our relationship, we used our voice mailboxes at work to leave lengthy messages. The majority of these are recorded onto tape to be preserved and listened to in times when we cannot be together. We have also entered the world of the Internet and other on-line services to maintain our communication.

Just as they needed speed for their communication, most couples rushed into love when they met face-to-face. Even though many years had passed since they last met, and even though their lives had changed in many ways, these lovers did not proceed slowly. Sixty-one percent of them reported that, on a scale of 1 (slow) to 5 (fast), compared to all their other relationships, this romance proceeded the fastest.

How fast is fast? One fourth of the survey participants resumed their Lost and Found Love within only a week of reconnecting, and an additional one fourth renewed their romances within the first three weeks. No wonder their relatives and friends worry!

Another 39% of the rekindlers waited up to a year before dating as a committed couple, and the rest waited longer. But those who waited before pursuing the romance were not going slowly to see what might develop—they *knew*. One woman in California, who reunited with her Lost Lover after forty-five years, wrote:

MY SON RECENTLY ASKED ME how long it took, after we met again, before I knew that "this was it." I thought awhile and answered, "About ten minutes."

The lovers' reasons for the lag between discovering their feelings and acting upon them depended on the circumstances. Some lovers were married, some were ill, some lived far apart. I do not remember any who said they waited because they were just being cautious. Even though one of the partners had most likely been hurt by the other person years before (sometimes seriously, as they themselves described in earlier parts of the questionnaire), they still seemed to jump right in. This is normal for these relationships, and not in itself a reason for their families and friends to be alarmed.

The Lost Love Project found dramatic emotional involvement. When participants compared their Lost and Found Loves to all of their other relationships, 71% indicated that this was their most emotional romance. Most often, it was the men who gushed about their deep love and respect for their partners, as did this man in his late thirties:

> JUST WANTED YOU TO KNOW that I have *never* been happier in *my entire life!* I owe it all to my Lost Lover. We both feel the same way—that being together is wonderful! We've been married ten years and still feel like we're on our honeymoon! *Seriously.* I have never been more relaxed, more secure, more honest, or more loved. Our marriage is very open, honest, and trustworthy. It's the neatest feeling in the whole world!
>
> In some ways we feel like we've always been together—that there wasn't a sixteen-year break. We really feel God had this plan for us. We definitely were meant to be together.

Given the strong feelings that they hold for their sweethearts, it should come as no surprise to find that even though they may have careers that require a high degree of logic, analytical ability, and pragmatism, when it comes to love, Lost and Found Lovers are hopeless romantics. Despite the many years the two lovers may have spent apart and the many times they may have changed residences, they saved mementos of their Lost Love. Nearly half of them saved letters, poems, and cards from their initial romances, even through subsequent relationships, including marriages. Another 43% saved gifts that the Lost Lovers had given them years ago, or saved souvenirs or memorabilia of the times they spent together. One woman wrote:

> THROUGH ALL THE YEARS AND through nine moves, I kept a little basket of letters, napkins with notes on them, notes, and stories that my Lost Lover, now my husband, had written to me over six years. When we reestablished contact, I copied over fifty pages of "stuff" and mailed it all to him. We call them our "Chronicles." I will forever treasure these letters from twenty years ago. In the last letter, before we each married other people, he told me we were the best of friends and that he would love me always, and who knew what the future would hold for us. His closing was, "Forever a part of you, Love, Dave."

Another 35% of these participants saved old records or music from their initial romances ("our song"), and 39% sent recordings (some people went out to buy them anew) of old songs through the mail to their newly rediscovered sweethearts. A college vice president wrote about her mementos:

> WE BEGAN A HEAVY-DUTY CORRESPONDENCE, and John sent me a recording of "Moon River" from *Breakfast at Tiffany's,* which we had seen and loved while we were dating initially. We exchanged current photographs, and in one the bracelet John had given me in college is visible on my wrist.

Even more commonly saved were photographs of the Lost Lover or of the two Lovers (68%). Sometimes they reported hiding these pictures from other lovers and spouses—in boxes, behind walls and fireplaces—or carrying them secretly in their wallets for years. Stories of rekindled lovers in the newspapers often include these old photos of the couples, along with their new, smiling pictures.

All of the rekindled romance's emotional intensity spills over into the bedroom. When asked to describe the intensity of the sexual involvement with their

Lost and Found Lovers compared to all other relationships, before or after, 63% of the participants said this was their most intense sexual relationship ever. The rating scale for this question went from 1 to 5, but 5 was not high enough for some people. They wrote down higher numbers, usually 10. Others made the same point by adding many exclamation points, as in these comments by a sixty-one-year-old man:

WE WERE BEST FRIENDS, AND we always said that the best feeling in the world is to be in love with the person who is in love with you. We always thought that no one in history had a love affair like we had. And the sex was the best that anyone in history had ever had!!!!!!!!!!!!

Some people added comments like "WOW!!" These responses seem even more impressive when we consider a recent poll by *Longevity* magazine: Married readers were asked if they considered their spouses to be their best-ever lovers. More than half of married men and women said no.

No matter what the age of the couple, rekindled lovers enjoy highly satisfying sexual relationships. It seems that Lost Lovers need not worry about whether they will be sexually appealing when they meet their former sweethearts again—even after the passage of time, extra pounds, baldness, wrinkles, or physical limitations. One woman in Canada who did worry told her reunion story:

OVER THE NEXT FEW MONTHS he called almost nightly. Our love was growing day by day. And then came May, his visit. We both knew we wanted to cross the line at that point. Love has never been made like that day! Here I am in my late thirties, a couple kids and a body that shows its age—fear and intimidation went through my mind. Do we leave the lights off? Yes! How can I get under the covers before he sees? Will I be "good" enough? Can I fake it? Pretty personal questions, eh?

Well, none of the above. Lights were bright with sunlight, and not an ounce of uncomfortable feelings were in that room. Faking anything was not an option.

The intensity was incredible—almost a spiritual awakening. We laughed and we cried and we shared each other more openly than we've ever done before.

A sizable group (10%) of participants checked a low intensity (1) of sexual involvement. But they were not suggesting that the Lost and Found Lover was a dud in bed. Instead, they wrote in the margins that they were not sexually active within their rekindled romances. A few were too ill, and a few older people were uninterested in this aspect of romance. One woman in her eighties commented about her Lost and Found Lover:

HE IS ALWAYS SO DEMANDING and at eighty-nine years old, I don't see why we should have to "play." I'm not interested in sexual relationships—I believe sex outside of marriage is not right. And I'm afraid of sexually transmitted diseases from him being intimate with his other women. But I value his friendship.

He never really appreciated me, so he would never marry me. He says marriages between races don't work. He's nuts—I've seen hundreds that work. I fell madly in love with him again and waited for a "miracle," but maybe it wasn't meant to be. Takes two to tango.

Many people who fit into this category were married to other partners, and they did not want to violate their marital fidelity by engaging in extramarital sex (although some of these couples admitted to "phone sex," "touching," or "petting"). One forty-year-old woman who did not include sex in her Lost and Found reunion wrote:

WE MET TWENTY YEARS AGO. He attended MIT and I lived in Florida. He was blown away by my string bikini and I was blown away by how brilliant he was. I was desperately in love with him. I adored him. He was the moon and the stars. I moved so we could live together, but he didn't want to commit. He never told me that he loved me. I suppose he never did.

I moved back to Florida and eventually married, but I never forgot about my first love—thought about him for years. He moved to Maine and got married—boy, was she ugly! We had no contact after that.

Then one night last year, I was using my computer on-line and checked for his name in the membership directory, and there he was! I e-mailed him. My CompuServe bills went from a few dollars to a few hundred. He flew down from Maine one day *for lunch,* just lunch! We kissed a lot, but I don't think I could handle sexual entanglements with him while being married to someone else.

I have no plans to leave my husband. He has been so good to me, and we have a very comfortable marriage. My Lost and Found Lover is in a miserable marriage, but that's his problem, not mine. I'm not going anywhere. But I'm having a great time enjoying this renewed friendship, and I'm truly amazed that we are friends again.

THE EXTRAMARITAL ROMANCES

Almost one third of the 1,001 couples in the Lost Love Project began their rekindled romances while they were married to others. In addition to the 30% who were married, another 11% called themselves separated, which might or might not be considered an extramarital beginning, depending on point of view. Also in the gray area for infidelity are those who reported living with a significant other (3%) and those who were engaged (1%) at the time they began their rekindled romances.

These answers report only on the person filling out the questionnaire. To keep the questionnaire short, the survey did not ask about the marital status of the Lost Lovers at the time of reconnection. If I had asked that question, I am convinced (from reading the details respondents wrote in the "comments" section) that the extramarital rate would have been much higher.

As might be expected, marital status makes a difference in whether the Lost and Found Lovers stay together—but not necessarily in the way one might expect. People who were married when they renewed romances were more likely to stay together with their Lost and Found Lovers than those who had been single when they reconnected. Roughly half (56%) of those who renewed the romance while they were single were still together at the time of the survey. In contrast, 76% of those who had been married when they reconnected were still together. The percentages were also high for those who had been living with a significant other (65%) or engaged (75%).

A very large percentage (79%) of those who reported that they were separated (as distinct from single) at the time of the renewed romance remained together, as did those who had been divorced when they reunited. Not surprisingly, those who were widowed had the highest success rate: 87% of them were still together.

One reason that fewer singles remained together might simply be their youth. One would expect the never-marrieds to be younger (and perhaps less experienced romantically and less emotionally mature) than those who had been married. Additionally, the fact that they had never chosen to make a long-term commitment might mean that they could not commit to their Lost Lovers, either.

The widows and widowers have the opposite characteristics in their favor: They are probably older than most of the Lost Love Project respondents (and thus more in touch with what they want in life), and they have made marital commitments that were broken only with the death of their spouses. It is not surprising that they are similarly loyal to their Lost Lovers as well.

The "Still Together" rekindled romances that began while the Lost Love Project respondents were clearly involved with others (i.e., they were married, engaged, or living with significant others) began as secret affairs. Some of them remain secret and extramarital. Some of these people telephoned me to tell me they feel torn between two loves and two lives. They do not want to hurt their spouses, whom they often profess still to love in many ways. Nor do they want to hurt their children by divorcing and dividing the family.

These callers are usually fifty-five and older. Because they grew up in a world where extramarital affairs were less common and more stigmatized than today, they feel ashamed of this secret, often unexpected, side of themselves revealed by their affair. Some reported that they are prominent and "upstanding" citizens of their communities but feel like frauds. One man confessed:

IT WAS AS IF THE brakes were released from common sense and common decency all at once. We commenced an incredible adulterous affair almost immediately.

Never in my wildest dreams would I have seriously considered what I was now doing routinely: writing sheaves of love letters, clandestine meetings, wild unrestrained sex, weekends out of town in other states, spending hundreds of hard-earned dollars at a whack in high-class restaurants and clubs. I gave her thousands of dollars to pay off urgent debts. Unbelievable, and yet true.

These people telephone me to talk, to cry, to ask about what is "normal" for my sample, and to request referrals to therapists. Usually it is the men who call; sometimes I talk to their confused Lost and Found Lovers as well. One letter came from a wounded wife:

A YEAR AGO, MY HUSBAND announced to me that he was in love, and always had been, with his high school sweetheart. They had been engaged, and he never got over being jilted. I knew about her before we married, and I was so happy that I made him forget her.

Somewhere in the thirty-five years of our marriage, he fell in love with her all over again. He would call her on her birthday every year even though she was married, too. They met a few times for dinner, then lost touch again. She eventually divorced her husband and when John found her again, he fell head over heels in love with her.

I confronted him. I had suspected something but never dreamed it had gone so far as an affair. He admitted it, and I left immediately. I got an apartment and a therapist.

We are not young people, and decisions had to be made for the good of the children, too. We are together again, but it isn't the same. Time is supposed to heal hurts, but it didn't heal John's hurt about being jilted, and it hasn't taken away my hurt in nine years. He says he doesn't love her anymore.

Can you tell me how someone can love a Lost Lover for almost thirty years, be married to someone else whom he loves out of respect and loyalty, but when the wife leaves he decides he really loves his wife? I can handle the memory of the girl before me, but I cannot handle the memory of the woman after me—and they are the same person.

I was his wife, but not the woman he wanted to spend his life with. I feel like I stepped into the middle of something and my gut feeling is that he still loves her. I need to understand. I don't want to go through life one phone call away from this woman.

Everyone knows, even the children. I still try to forgive him on a daily basis. When I can get through a whole day that I don't think about it, I'll know I'm getting better. I'm in the anger stage of loss. I try not to throw it in his face—he has been kind and understanding, but he's tired of talking about it.

There are a lot of us hurt spouses out there. Hopefully your study will help someone like me understand.

The rekindlers have shared with me how their romances began: Usually the Lost Lover who was single, separated, divorced, or widowed contacted the other Lost Lover in friendship, or with the hope that the former sweetheart was also free to rekindle their love. When that Lost Lover turned out to be married, engaged, or living with someone, and thus unavailable, the two former lovers got together for lunch or dinner anyway, just to reminisce about old times. One woman, who met her Lost Lover for a drink when he was in town, wrote:

WE TALKED TILL THEY CLOSED the bar. It was so incredibly comfortable—a word we would use over and over again. When I drove him back to his hotel, on impulse or habit he leaned over and kissed me goodnight, then stepped out of the car and out of my life.

I couldn't sleep that night. I was so confused by that kiss. Up until then, I thought we were two old high school chums talking over old times and catching up on each other's lives. That kiss really threw me.

Unable to stand it any longer, I called him at six A.M. and asked what that kiss meant. He seemed as confused as I was. Said he wasn't sure, either, but he would write to me. Within four days I had a note from him saying he was coming through my town and wanted to see me—"We have to talk."

We met, we talked. We both felt something that evening, how incredibly comfortable it was. Like slipping on an old shoe. We agreed we weren't sure where we were heading, but we wanted to see more of each other. We did, even though we lived 300 miles apart, even though he was married. I would never have dreamed of seeing any other married man, and he said he had never been unfaithful to his wife in thirty-two years.

We soon began meeting at motels. The intensity of this relationship was something neither of us had ever experienced before. We thought about each other constantly, we plotted and schemed to find ways to be together. We were like magnets, and when we were within six feet of each other, we couldn't keep our hands off each other. We wrote daily, and called when we could.

Being apart was intolerable. He couldn't get me out of his head to make his marriage work. He told his wife that he needed some time alone. He told her about me. By the time he got home a week later, his wife had told all the children. He called me that night to tell me he had agreed to break off all contact with me.

He went for marriage counseling with his wife, but deep down he wanted to be with me. He finally told his wife he wanted a divorce, and he moved out. When the divorce was completed, we married.

I can't find enough superlatives to describe this marriage and this relationship. He fills needs in me that haven't been met in my whole life! He has been a godsend for my daughters, and his children now accept me as a friend, although that was very difficult for them in the beginning.

We are so grateful that we found each other again after a separation of thirty-five years, and we find ourselves frequently telling each other, "I'm so glad you're here!!"

In most cases, the spouse knows of the initial meeting and doesn't mind. In fact, the spouse may even join in the initial reunion. The Lost Lovers expect only a few hours of innocent talk. They are not prepared for the sparks between them! What started in innocence becomes too precious to lose again, and the two are drawn into a romance against their better judgment.

The sexual aspect of these affairs does not begin casually, and it does not continue casually. There is a good deal of soul-searching before they proceed, and some of these Lost and Found Lovers say they agonize over their love every day. One man who read a newspaper article about my research sent me a completely anonymous note—with not even a first name or return address:

I HAVE NEVER GONE THROUGH so much hell in my life, as wanting to see and be with her. I am going through all the guilt feelings about my wife and kids, plus wanting to be with her. It's not very much fun at all, but I have such deep feelings for her, and it's almost like the forty-year break never happened, once I saw her again.

She certainly doesn't look the same. She is a little chubby and older, but when I see her, I see the fifteen-year-old girl I used to cherish. It's so hard to explain to anyone.

I never dreamed in a million years that this was going to happen to me. I have never looked for an affair and have never had one in thirty-five years of marriage. It is the farthest thing from my mind and always has been. I'm just not like that.

But when I met her again, I fell for her all over again, and am half sick thinking about her all the time. I wonder if it will ever go away this time. I enjoyed your article, because I thought I was alone with this lovesick feeling that I have for her. I feel so guilty and the article helped me deal better with it.

It is so dangerous contacting an old flame from years ago, trust me . . . it's like playing with fire.

If they have entered into these relationships at all, the lovers intend to remain together for life, one way or another. Some are waiting to achieve financial independence before they divorce their spouses and marry their Lost and Found Lovers. Some are waiting until their children are grown. Several women confessed that one or more children from their present marriages have secretly been fathered by the Lost and Found Lovers! One Lost Lover has found some peace within her extramarital situation:

> MY LOST LOVER IS STILL married. When we first were involved it lasted eight years. Since then ten years have passed. We have learned that what is important is the time spent together. We can laugh, cry, read, touch, share, eat, shower, or any other thing. We are happy to be together, but able to be apart.
>
> We both know that our financial status affords us freedom that other people in similar circumstances may not have. Corporate credit cards, company cars, business trips . . . these are available to use to disguise our time together. We make full use of them.

Another common reason for extramarital rekindled romances is that some of these older Lost Lovers are bearing the responsibility for very ill spouses. Although their marriages have essentially been destroyed by the severity of these physical disorders, the Lost Lovers do not abandon their spouses. One sixty-five-year-old man wrote of the following hardships:

> THIS LOST LOVE RELATIONSHIP HAS included the happiest moments of my whole life, including the most beautiful, wonderful— and every other superlative—sexual fulfillment. It has helped me immeasurably to retain my physical and mental health through a very stressful period of my life.
>
> My Lost Lover and I are still in unhappy marital situations which are further complicated by my Lost Lover giving devoted care to her frail father, and my caring for and nursing my wife who has physical

disabilities and psychiatric problems caused by an accident several years ago.

I can only take two "respite breaks" each year. I believe you will understand the longing and yearning that we feel during the long months of separation. At these times our lifeline is the daily telephone calls, letters, and cards, enabling us to help each other through each day, until we can be permanently together.

Never in my wildest dreams did I think that it was possible for a man and a woman at "our time of life" to have been privileged to find and experience such emotional and physical happiness together.

Another man wrote to share the following story:

TWO YEARS AGO I RECEIVED a phone call out of the blue from my Lost Lover who had been lost to me for over forty-five years. She explained to me that for three or four years she had been dreaming of me, that I was calling for help. She called my aunt, a former neighbor of hers when she was a girl, and found out my wife was far along in the course of Alzheimer's disease, got my phone number, and called me. I have no reason to doubt her story. Her letters and phone calls were of tremendous support to me as I gave almost total care to my wife for another year, until she entered a rest home. I visit daily when I am home.

We had dated during World War II. Our parting was sudden and traumatic caused by a lack of communication—a desire of each of us to have a career that we hadn't discussed. When we met again, she had been widowed for twenty-five years and had not remarried. We traveled together for a few weeks, and this was a delightful time for us both.

Her brother and his wife are very friendly to me, but my sister does not accept the situation at all. My mother-in-law and father-in-law are understandably not too gung ho about my relationship with my Lost Lover, but we manage to get along in cooperation. People who have any experience with Alzheimer's disease tend to be very sympathetic to my plight and are accepting of my relationship with my Lost Lover, who I joyfully accept as Found Lover! I cannot commit bigamy, nor would I get a divorce, but I do not feel guilty about loving and accepting love from another, since I can never again be with my wife in that kind of a relationship. It is difficult to love two women at the same time, but I do, in far different ways!

Some of the people who participated in the Lost Love Project had already left their marriages to be with their Lost and Found Lovers openly and full time. Almost all of these couples are now married to each other. Most of them report that they had been in dysfunctional marriages at the time they reconnected with their Lost Lovers, and have never been happier than in their new Lost and Found marriages. The marriages formed by the Lost and Found Lovers have stronger and deeper bonds, are more loving and passionate, and—perhaps ironically— are reported to be more religious or "spiritual" than the original marriages.

So rekindled romances do break apart marriages, that is true. Spouses and children are hurt (and so are the lovers), and their pain should be acknowledged even as we applaud the fairy tale endings for these renewed romances. One woman captured these contradictory feelings:

MY LOST LOVER AND I have often discussed this remarkable emotional bond, and tried to find something written on the subject. In fact, we've speculated that there may be relatively little discussion of the phenomenon because it is often antifamily, iconoclastic, countersocial in that it may result in broken marriages, upset stabilities, impulsive upheavals in previously settled relationships.

The power of the Lost Love bond is enormous. To my mind it is a social steamroller. I do not think it can be stopped in its inexorable course. Any writer who wants to report on these romances must figure out how to talk about these circumstances without appearing to condone some of the damage that can result. How, for example, does one discuss the dilemma of having to balance serving oneself against disrupting a steady-state relationship? From my point of view as a person immersed in the dilemma, I must say it is unenviable, but there is only one answer. One simply does not deny the love of one's life—there is only one of them.

It is naive and unrealistic to believe that former lovers—especially first loves—can meet just once, to reminisce casually about old times, that former romantic feelings no longer exist, or that these feelings can be controlled by love or loyalty to a spouse. The first reconnection is far from ordinary, and like potato chips, just one is never enough. Assume that sexual feelings will surface. So, a Lost Lover in a marriage that he or she values should think twice before "doing lunch."

COURTLY LOVERS

As we have seen, these 1,001 Lost and Found Lovers are highly emotional. The "up" side to this is the passion they bring into these love relationships. The "down" side is that they can be an obsessive bunch. For example, 71% of the Lost Love Project participants admitted to thinking about the lost lover constantly. One twenty-two-year-old woman wrote:

> I AM STILL VERY MUCH in love with my Lost Lover, but he's with someone new. I think of him all the time. Even when I make love to the person I am with now, I think of my Lost Lover. I'll never be able to let him go. I send letters, but he never writes back. If there is any way to get over him, please help me to do so!

Twenty-nine percent had trouble eating or sleeping, and 18% reported that they became jealous of time spent apart. These characteristics come right out of the songs of the troubadours and Eleanor of Aquitaine's rules for courtly love which we discussed in Chapter Three.

These responses mirrored the lovers' depth of commitment during the renewed romance. Couples who stayed together were significantly more likely to report excessive, intrusive thinking and behavior patterns than the couples who parted again. And as I studied the questionnaire results, it became obvious that these couples were more deeply involved during their rekindled romances than during their initial love. Although 46% of the participants reported dating without being sexually involved when they described their first romance, only 25% described their rekindled romances that way. Sixty-nine percent said their rekindled romances included sexual involvement, as compared to 48% of the initial loves.

But these renewed relationships are not just sexual flings. They are committed relationships, even though they might not last. For example, at some point, about 30% of rekindled lovers lived together, but only 7% did so originally. Thirty percent of rekindled lovers got engaged, but only 10% did so in their original relationship. And even though 6% of the lovers got married originally, 33% did so the second time around.

Even when they do not marry, these Lost and Found Loves are quite successful the second time around. Only 14% of all couples have had no contact at all. Another 9% say they write or call but do not see each other (sometimes only because of distance and expense). Some remain friends but are not sexually involved (8%). One man in Canada wrote about his Lost Love friendship:

JAN AND I MET WHEN we were fifteen. We were both lucky enough to spend our childhood summers in naive and idyllic splendour on a wonderful lake. Her family owned an island and my family had been in the area for over fifty years.

We were together for three years, and we were each other's first loves. We spent hours reading Dylan Thomas, Hemingway, and Proust to each other. Our relationship seemed so much more mature than the other teenage flings.

Our relationship ended on the dock at her cottage, and to this day I really don't know why.

A few years ago, I went on a sentimental journey in my canoe on that lake. I paddled to the place where I learned to swim, past our old family cottage, and across the water I saw her cottage. But I had not heard from Jan in more than twenty-five years. It was fall and no cottagers were around. I took a chance and wrote a note to her and placed it between the plates of glass in what used to be her bedroom.

I heard nothing through winter and spring and did not give it much thought. Then in May I got an answer to my note. Jan's cousin is now owner of the cottage. She found the note and forwarded it to Jan.

We have now been writing to each other for over five years. She had harboured a lot of rage against me based on some misunderstandings of our time together, and we have been able to heal this through the letters. She has achieved heights of fulfillment as a wife, mother, and teacher.

I have traveled to Toronto and have met her wonderful family. Each Christmas, I am happy to send presents for everyone in the house.

But for some people, a friendship does not necessarily mean that the Lost and Found Lover is a platonic buddy. For example, one woman added a note:

WELL, IT'S NOT EXACTLY A friendship; it's more like some strange sort of relative with a sexual charge.

Others echoed her, admitting that they did not rule out a romantic relationship in the future. A woman in her thirties gave the following characterization:

MY LOST LOVER AND I both feel as though we are soul mates, meant to be together. But I am married. This situation tears us up, because my husband is really a wonderful person. My husband and I are good friends and have had many happy years together, and we are committed to our children's emotional well-being. My Lost and Found Lover respects that.

While I do love my husband, it is not the same intense, "in love" feeling that I feel for my first love. But my husband is very good to me and values our marriage. I care about him a lot and feel as though I owe it to my children to keep our family together.

The problem is that I can't bring myself to let my Lost and Found Lover go again. I listed him here as a "friend," because we are not sexual together, but he is so much more. I truly feel torn right down the middle.

Many others describe themselves currently as lovers (21%). Another 7% report that they now live together, and these are not necessarily young couples who look upon this as a trial marital situation. One woman in her fifties told me:

> WE BEGAN OUR RELATIONSHIP IN the sixth grade! We were inseparable. We were obsessive about each other. As we grew into our teens, he was going down the wrong road fast and loved me too much to ruin my life, so I finally gave up on him (at eighteen) and married someone else. He never married and always loved me.
>
> He feels like he hit the lottery, getting me back. I divorced after sixteen years, but didn't get back with him until twenty years later. We get along great—we are best friends and lovers. We will be together forever. He doesn't do the "M" word.

Fully 72% of all the participants checked "We Are Still Together" to describe their current relationship with their Lost and Found Lovers. To understand just how high the figure is, consider this: If you meet someone new tomorrow and begin dating, will you have a 72% chance of staying together?

STAYING TOGETHER

The Lost and Found Lovers who stay together differ in significant ways from those who break up. First of all, very few people who were still together had rekindled a romance with more than one Lost Lover. They chose to reconnect with one and only one special person in their past. Moreover, if they had been involved with that special person when they were seventeen or younger they were more likely to be together with him or her than those who had met at an older age. The likeliest of all couples (76%) to remain together were those who had been first loves, (compared to only 64% for later loves).

Those who dated without sexual involvement during the initial romance were significantly more likely to be together (80%) than those who had dated with sexual involvement (71%). One man, who first met his Lost Lover in 1949, pointed out the significance of this platonic stage:

> ANN AND I KNOW THAT somehow those early teen years bonded us in a special way for life. I want to stress that the bonding occurred without sex, or at least without intercourse in those early years. We were together virtually every day and most evenings without performing the sex act. We did a lot of cuddling. I think your research is going to show the importance of this type of courtship between men and women.

Although 71% of the Lost and Found Lovers who had been engaged during the first romance were still together, lovers who had lived together during the first romance were least likely to remain together (54%) after reconnecting. Even those who married and divorced each other the first time had a better success rate than that: When they reconnected, the previously married couples stayed together 67% of the time. This is food for thought for all those who believe a marriage has a better chance of survival if the couple lives together first. It was not true for these rekindlers, and recent psychological research has shown that it is not true for first-time couples, either.

The couples who married during their rekindled romances stayed married. Only fifteen people reported that they had divorced each other. Considering the national divorce rate of roughly 50% for first marriages and 60% for second marriages, these couples are doing extraordinarily well.

None of the reasons for the initial breakups, including parental disapproval, had any bearing on whether the rekindled couple would stay together the second time around. This information might help future parents allow their children the responsibility for their own romances, although offering parental opinions and words of caution is certainly important.

Those who waited twenty-one to twenty-five years or longer before they rekindled their romances were significantly more likely to remain together than those who reconnected earlier. The nostalgia that finds its way into the middle years seems to support these romances.

The Lost and Found Lovers who indicated the fastest beginning to the renewed romances after their first meetings, and the greatest emotional and sexual intensity, as compared to all their other relationships, were significantly more likely to stay together.

The couples who stayed together purchased significantly more gifts, traveled more frequently to see each other, and wrote more letters than rekindlers who broke up, even though they did not necessarily spend excessive money doing so. They were also much more likely than couples who broke up to have saved old gifts, music, photos, and souvenirs from their first romance—and to have shared them with each other when they renewed their love.

These shared memories no doubt help explain why the rekindlers still together reported that they recaptured old aspects of themselves, and felt young again, significantly more often than couples who separated a second time.

To sum up, of the Lost and Found Lovers who reported that they were still together, almost a third of them are currently married to their Lost and Found Lovers. Another 7% live together, and 7% are currently engaged. Another 21% described themselves as lovers. The remainder of the Lost and Found Lovers who are together may still meet as friends, or keep in touch by telephone and letters. The numbers clearly indicate success the second time around.

LOST AND FOUND—AND LOST AGAIN

Just as renewed romances get off to a flying start as compared to other romances, they end faster if a couple is fated to part again. More than three fourths of the Lost and Found Lovers who broke up again reported that their second romances were shorter than the initial relationships. Unfortunately, this did not mean that they recovered any faster. In fact, the emotional recovery time for the rekindled romance was longer for 98% of the couples than the recovery time for their first relationship.

Losing a Lost and Found Lover for the second time can be devastating and should not be compared to an ordinary breakup. The participants wrote that they worried about their long grieving period, and that relatives and friends criticized them for healing so slowly. It obviously takes a long time for people who have gone through Lost and Found and Lost Again Love relationships to recover. They (and their families, friends, and therapists) must be patient with their need to grieve.

One reason for the depth of their grief may be that many people in this group had chosen *which* relationship to rekindle, no doubt because they deeply believed that it would work the second time. The fact that it did not work was a huge letdown and led to a feeling of personal failure.

Contrary to common beliefs, old problems did not usually come back to haunt these romances. Although four romances ended because the couples still had different expectations or lived too far apart, almost all of the second breakups occurred for reasons different from the reasons for the first breakups. The most common reason was other relationships: 5% of the 1,001 couples could not leave a marriage or significant other. Three couples were now sexually incompatible. One woman in her thirties, a magazine entertainment critic, described her rekindled romance attempt:

MY RELATIONSHIP WITH MY LOST Lover has been a source, at different times, of strength, frustration, longing, and satisfaction. The fact that it ended when I found out that he was pursuing a gay lifestyle adds an interesting twist! We are still friends.

The fact that the relationship is no longer viable has freed me in many ways. He made me realize I cannot look to anyone else to fulfill needs relating to self-esteem and self-worth. But still . . . what a trip! Sometimes I think it would make a great movie.

Other reasons varied widely (see Appendix III). Although one might expect career conflicts to be significant now that these lovers are older, only ten of the couples had career conflicts, usually because they were unable to relocate to be near each other. The second time around, only two relationships ended because of parental disapproval. But this does not mean that the parents gave up *trying* to influence their grown children. One fifty-year-old woman, now living with her Lost and Found Lover, wrote:

WHEN WE WERE YOUNG, WE lived together in bliss for a few months before his mother broke us up. She was Catholic and felt her son and his ex-wife should try again to make a life for their young son. He went back to his ex-wife briefly and miserably, and I, devastated, returned to my family, heartbroken and vowing never to feel for another man the same as I did for my Lost Lover.

I never forgot him, and over the years I wondered what might have been. After sixteen years, I contacted him and we got back together. We are both happier now than ever and very content. His mother *still* interferes, hoping and praying that she can somehow once again break us up.

Three percent of the romances ended this time because of different expectations. This was the reason that the first love couples gave most often. The first loves who separated did not check "Couldn't Leave a Marriage or Significant Other," despite the fact that the extramarital affairs almost always occurred between first loves!

Whatever the reasons for the second breakup, it is very hard to convince Lost and Found Lovers that a relationship is truly over. After all, if a lover can return once, why not again, and again, and again? When the respondents were asked, "If you are separated from your Lost Lover now, does it feel as if your relationship is permanently over?" fewer than half of those whose rekindled romances had ended answered yes.

Even more people answered no, including some widows and widowers. And 11% are just not sure what will happen in the future. For these couples, it's not even over when the fat lady sings. As one young woman wrote:

ALTHOUGH THE ROMANCE DID NOT work the second time, I still think we may end up together. When we are together, there is nothing better. We have so much in common and know each other so well that I couldn't imagine either of us being with anyone else. Because we are both young—I'm twenty-three and he is twenty-six—and graduating college this year, I think a lot of our problems will go away. For now I'm content to talk to him on the phone once a month or so. I have begun to date others and am realizing how special my former boyfriend really is.

A man in his late fifties had different reasons for feeling uncertain:

WE WERE HIGH SCHOOL SWEETHEARTS. As graduation drew near our relationship began to deteriorate due to the incessant inter-ference and pressure from her father, who obviously did not approve.

I elected to enter the U.S. Navy and she continued her education. It didn't take long to receive the proverbial "Dear John" letter. Al-though it didn't come as a big surprise, I was devastated.

Some twenty-nine years later we were reunited. In all that time no one ever really took her place. During the period when we were reunited I suffered from a complete lack of trust. This emotion even-tually became so strong I thought it would consume me, so I elected to break off the relationship.

I could not talk to her about this feeling and to this day she doesn't know. I don't know about trying again and forgiving in the future, but I know I can't forget.

WAS IT WORTHWHILE?

Even Lost and Found Lovers who did not stay together felt their rekindled romances had been worthwhile. Almost half of the participants reported that they felt better about the past after talking about it as a couple. One man in his fifties had carried around a lot of guilt—and his Lost Lover had carried a lot of anger—that dissipated when they discussed why their initial romance broke down right before the wedding:

MY CONTACTING HER AFTER TWENTY-NINE years was not because I was nuts or drunk or impulsive (male menopause, maybe), but it's something I needed to resolve or close before we both pass away! No loving relationship should end the way ours did, ninety days before the wedding. I went to her apartment once with flowers to apologize personally but no one would open the door. She was angry and afraid of me.

I really blew it with her with the things I said and did. In retrospect, I am surprised she stayed with me as long as she did! I wanted her to know she did nothing to make me not love her. My actions caused the problems. And the way it ended has been my dilemma—my feelings haven't lessened over the years. It's been a painful piece of my life. My apologies were long overdue.

One third of the respondents were finally able to free themselves from recurring fantasies about their lost lovers. One woman in her thirties wrote:

I STARTED THE INITIAL ROMANCE a few days after my dad died. I guess I transferred a lot of my needs to this guy, and that is why it felt unbearable to break up—because I would have to grieve my dad's death. Finally I moved across the country to get away from him.

After about thirteen years, I let myself go back to see him and finish it. I was ready and willing to spend a weekend with him, but it didn't happen and I was sixteen all over again—the heartache, disappointment, and incredible sadness and pain.

When I told my brother about this, he pointed out that *nothing* had changed—that even years ago my Lost Lover used to back out of commitments with me all the time. But I had never noticed that pattern until that day when our renewed romance plans fell through.

And after a short while (short! maybe a week), I was free. Something in me shifted, or woke up, and I was done—the dreams stopped—everything was over with him.

Similarly, a man in his thirties stated:

WE MET ONLY TWICE AFTER contact was reestablished. I very quickly learned that either she had changed remarkably for the worse, or she was never the perfect woman I had remembered. The realization that I did not want any further contact with her absolutely set a large part of my heart free. My memories of her had made it difficult to be happy in my marriage, which ended after two years.

Almost one half of the Lost Love Project participants realized, because of the rekindled romance, that their initial relationships could not have worked then.

One third of the respondents found it to be worthwhile to hear why the Lost Lover left the first time. This was particularly true for the first loves, who may have had trouble communicating when they were young.

Many people (43%) valued the opportunity to make amends, as in this story told by a woman in her fifties:

I NEVER LOVED ANOTHER MAN the way I loved and love this man. (The current relationship is a more mature kind of love.) It also was and is the best sexual relationship I ever had. After his wife divorced him, he called to meet me for lunch, because he felt a need to "make amends." We were immediately attracted to each other as strongly as before. We married on Valentine's Day six months later, and we're very happy.

More than one half of the participants said that the rekindled romance was worthwhile because they were able to recapture the past and old aspects of themselves, and 49% experienced feeling young again. This was especially true for first love couples. One man described the nostalgia he felt on his first Lost and Found "date":

WE HADN'T SEEN EACH OTHER or heard from each other in thirty-nine years. She told me to meet her at her father's home, about one hour's drive from my home, and so I drove there two weeks later. I met her at the door, and the effect was electrifying. But I held back my emotions for the moment (after all, her father had thrown me out when she was fifteen).

We drove to some favorite haunts . . . dunes, beaches, a nearby resort town, and a memorable spot that was the site of our first kiss. I was speechless. I was afraid to even touch her. When she kissed me there, I was overwhelmed. An aging schoolboy on his first date! Later, when I took her home (she had told her dad we would be home by 9:30! Nothing changes!) we had a long embrace, and she walked me to my car, where we kissed again. I drove home in a daze.

It's been a real storybook romance since then. She was fifty-eight and I was sixty-three when I found her again.

The questionnaires revealed that just as many couples no longer together found their rekindled romances to be worthwhile—for one or more of the reasons listed on the survey—as those who were still together.

It's clear that no matter how the relationship turned out, most people would not hesitate to try to renew it. More than half of the people in the Lost Love Project (53%) wrote that they would choose to renew the relationship again if they could. One man in his fifties, who currently has no contact at all with his Lost Lover, affirmed this:

WE ARE THROUGH FOR NOW, but she has been running around in my brain for the past thirty-nine years and that won't ever cease. I will wait for her forever.

While 53% represents a large part of the sample, it is not the whole story: Another 13% of the participants—all of them still together with their Lost and Found Lovers—left this question blank, thinking it only applied to people who were not together anymore. They assumed their answers would be obvious: *Of course I would!* They put "not applicable" or "N/A" next to the question. One woman who left this question blank described her marriage:

WE ARE THE CLICHÉD SOUL mates. We read each other's minds. It doesn't matter that thirty-three years were in between. We are happier than we have ever been. He brings me roses from the garden every day. He calls me from work. Or he checks in with me in the house if we are at home and we haven't talked for awhile.

AND THE SEX!!!!!!!!! We have a saying, the grass will die, the laundry will pile up, etc.

We should have been together the first time, but when you are young you sometimes do not recognize the real thing. Although I do wonder what might have happened, you just have to live with what you have and boy do we love what we have. We cuddle and spend our free time with each other by choice.

We have been married over six years, and I am still his bride. I know I always will be. I really love this man, gray hair and all! Whew. Love at age sixteen is still going strong at fifty-four.

So I'm convinced that, if they had it to do over, 66% of the Lost Love Project participants would go for it! One woman, delightedly married to her Lost and Found Lover for almost twenty-five years, had these words of advice:

THANK YOU FOR STUDYING THIS important subject. People don't believe us when we say we are not newlyweds. They envy us our relationship and love for each other. Maybe they should follow suit, right?

My old flame;
I can't even think of his name,
And I'll never be the same
Until I discover what became
Of my old flame.

JOHNSTON AND COSLOW, "My Old Flame"

THE LYRICS TO THIS song from 1934 are still heartbreakingly true. Some people do keep yearning for Lost Lovers, and even searching for them, though they may not even remember their Lost Lovers' names.

One morning, as I was looking over my mail in the Psychology Department mailroom, I heard someone call my name. I turned and saw a middle-aged man standing at the door. He asked if I had time to talk to him in my office. I had a class to teach within a few minutes, so I asked him to return during my office hours, when I would be happy to see him. Clearly disappointed, he launched into a quick version of his situation: He had learned about my Lost Love Project and asked if I could help him find a woman who had attended California State University at Sacramento with him almost twenty years earlier. Although I told him that I do not reunite people, he kept right on talking. He was clearly in turmoil, so I listened.

The woman had been a psychology major, as had he, and he sat next to her in many of their classes. They studied together sometimes, and even went out on a few dates. I suggested that our college alumni association would probably forward a letter to her, if they had her current address. Then she could, if she chose, contact him. I told him that that had worked for me. No, he said, the alumni association had already told him they could not find her, because he did not know her name. No last name, no first name, not even initials. It was a long time ago, he said. But how, I asked, did he think *I* could find her without a name? He admitted that he really had no idea.

This was not the only time people asked me to find nameless past loves. Other Searchers knew the name but not the spelling, or had very sketchy information about where the Lost Lovers might be. So they sent me photographs of their Lost Lovers as they appeared years ago. A few writers described their Lost Lovers' physical characteristics (in case I might happen to run into these people in my daily travels):

> HE STANDS ABOUT SIX FEET three inches and the last I knew weighed one hundred forty to one hundred sixty pounds. He has dark brown hair, and a "hare lip" on the left side.

Despite all of my efforts to stress in radio and television interviews that I was conducting psychological research on Lost and Found Lovers who had already been reunited, many people wrote to me after my appearances to ask me to find their Lost Lovers. Often they had tuned in during the middle of the interview and had not heard the description of the study.

Once I appeared on a national talk show that inaccurately labeled me on screen as someone who reunites Lost Lovers. Of course this caused a flood of letters from people of all ages. I wrote back to all of them, telling them about the purpose of my Lost Love Project, and explaining that I was not reuniting anyone. Sometimes I wrote a short note at the bottom of the letter, suggesting easy methods of relocating missing people, such as asking a former employer, school, or family member of the Lost Lover to forward a letter.

When I learned that this talk show would be rerun two months later, I asked the producers to correct the labeling. The correction accurately explained the purpose of my research, but I received just as many letters as before asking me to find Lost Lovers. One man definitely overestimated the size of the Lost Love Project's staff (I am it), as well as its purpose; he must have assumed that I had personally reunited all the couples in my study:

AFTER SEEING A REPRESENTATIVE FROM your organization on *Leeza,* I felt that you might be able to assist me.

Approximately thirty-two years ago I attended a summer camp in New Hampshire. It was a Lutheran Church camp. While attending this camp I met a girl by the name of [name deleted]. She is the very first girl I ever had a crush on. After attending this camp, we wrote to each other a number of times, but for some reason we stopped. The last I heard she resided in Cambridge, Massachusetts.

I attempted to contact her through the Cambridge Lutheran Church, but had no luck doing so. I made this attempt a couple of years ago. But since seeing *Leeza,* and seeing what your organization is capable of doing, I thought I would give it one last chance. I don't even know if she would remember me.

My guess, based on the Lost Love Project, is that she would remember him very well. Will some woman read this and recognize that she fits his description?

Although I was unable to help these people locate their Lost Lovers, I found many of their letters especially touching because they were written by seniors wanting to do a "life review," to make amends, or to gain a sense of closure before they die. One woman wrote:

I AM VERY EMBARRASSED TO write this because I am seventy-three years of age and should have no thoughts of the past, but I do.

My high school sweetheart and I broke up when he caught me sitting in the park with another young man. My Lost Lover had come to the United States from Germany before World War II to live with his uncle.

He worked after school at a supermarket, where I first met him. He later went on to attend school at Columbia University. I had no contact with him until we bumped into each other at a train station in the fifties. It was heaven to see him. We sat next to each other on the train and caught up with all the missing years.

We met secretly the next day and realized we were still very much in love. But we were both very much married with several children.

We were going to meet again the next day. I wanted to meet and be with him so very badly but I saw no future so I never showed up for the date. I wish now that I had at least given him a phone number.

All I wish to know is if he is alive and well. I will always love him, but I certainly can contain my feelings. I would never cause any problems or embarrassment to him or myself.

My husband died ten years ago. I have beautiful grown children and grandchildren. I would love to say hello to my Lost Lover and talk on the phone as friends.

I would appreciate any way you could inform me or help me locate him. I haven't told anyone about this letter. My kids would think Mom has lost her mind.

Many people, divorced or widowed, were seeking their Lost Lovers in hopes of rekindling their romances:

MY LOST LOVE WAS A long time ago, and I've never forgotten it, and would give anything to locate him and revive our friendship after all these years.

I went to his graduation from Tulane University in 1950 and went with him to his prom. The whole experience was wonderful and I was very much in love with him, and he was with me. I went to college in Chicago and he went on to graduate work in Boston. I wrote him a "Dear John" letter that I've always regretted.

Anyway, can you help me find him and get in touch with him again after all these years? I'm a widow and would just love to know if he's okay, happy, and possibly still interested in an old flame.

I'm sixty-one years old and I know it's a long time and I would probably shock him. He is sixty-four or sixty-five now. Thanks.

Perhaps these efforts by single-again Searchers indicate that Lost Lovers can be tucked into the corners of our minds as "back-up plans" until useful. For example:

EVEN THOUGH HE NEVER RETURNED my call this time, I am glad he has my phone number again. I keep hoping, should anything happen (a divorce, he becomes a widower, etc.), that he'll know where to find me and call me right away!

Reading about your research renews my hope that it's possible that we might see each other again. It makes me realize that I'm not as silly as some people think; that other people think about their first loves, too, and often go out and find each other, sometimes with wonderful results.

Should you ever decide to do any writing about those who "pine and wait," please contact me. AND if my good old Lost Lover ever does come back into my life, I just may write to you again!

A very similar letter came from a man in his sixties:

RECENTLY I BEGAN TO THINK of her more and more often, and have dreams about her. She is always as inaccessible in my dreams as in real life. It was like I was falling in love with her all over again, sight unseen, which is foolish to the extreme. Sometimes these feelings are so intense as to almost bring me to tears.

Anyway, I wrote to her a few months after I learned her address. She never answered. She is likely a happily married grandmother, perhaps with little remembrance of me. But one never knows.

If I were granted one wish in this world, it wouldn't be for fame, wealth, or power. It would be to successfully reconnect with my Lost Lover in this or another lifetime.

So this is the end of my story. Maybe if you write a book, you'll have a category for people like me: people who go through life secretly yearning for an old flame. I wonder how many of us there are in this country and around the world?

Of course, you are more than welcome to use any of the above story should you choose to include a chapter about open-ended yearning for old love. Then perhaps she will read your book, recognize herself, and know how cherished her memory is to me.

People in their mature years often look for different characteristics in a partner than what they found desirable when they were young—hence this late-life search for the boy who was only a "nice guy" years ago, or "just a friend":

I HAVE LOST TRACK OF someone special from my past and certainly hope that you will be of some assistance to me. He was a special friend I met in Japan in 1962 when we were both in eighth grade. Our fathers were stationed there in the Air Force.

Eventually he quit school and joined the Navy. Both of our fathers were then in Vietnam. His mother had to have a bilateral mastectomy, so he came back and took care of his younger brothers and sisters. Much to my surprise, he took me out for a burger (I was by then engaged to someone else) and proposed marriage!! Although I had, and still have, a profound soft spot in my heart for him, I turned him down with the usual explanations of "just friends."

For many years I have wondered if he served in Vietnam and most of all, did he return? What has happened to this kind, thoughtful, sensitive human being? Is he happy?

I married, have grown children and grandchildren as well. I am now single. Should you, by some great streak of luck, locate [name deleted], you may give him my address and phone number. P.S. He knows me as the *bright* redhead.

Others were seeking closure of the Lost Love romance, as this woman wrote:

MY STORY BEGAN IN THE late forties, as playmates, and a friendship turned into a first love in the fifties. There is something special about first love that lives in our hearts and the backs of our minds.

He joined the Navy, and as life goes I married and had a baby. This marriage did not last. I saw him again after that in 1957, and we dated a few times, but again we lost each other until 1968 when we spent eight wonderful days together reliving our young days together. We talked about old times and the future, but again we lost each other and both went on to other marriages. Mine lasted only two years.

In 1973, I heard from an old school friend that my Lost Lover had returned from Alaska, but we have not made contact. I have been through cancer with two operations, and I have found myself thinking about my Lost Lover. I would like to hear from him and talk to him to put closure to our Lost Young Love.

hope she finds him. And I certainly hope they stay together the next time!

Another woman was seeking closure more of her obsessive thoughts than of her actual feelings about her Lost Lover, a musician in a well-known band in Europe:

I LOST CONTACT WITH SOMEONE I love and can't get out of my mind. He is in my thoughts ALL the time and it is really killing me inside. I pray every day that I'll find him again. My feelings haven't changed and it has affected me in ways no one can understand. I've tried to have relationships and even almost convinced myself I was over him and in love with someone new. I hurt this new man in my life in ways that I never realized I could, and I'm truly sorry for that. I hoped that I could "replace" my Lost Lover [name deleted], but no one could. I imagined I was with him when I was with anyone else.

I really need to find him, talk to him, see him. I need PEACE in my life! I'm tired of crying at night, or driving down the road listening to a song that reminds me of what we shared. I've saved all his letters, phone messages, and every journal note I ever wrote about him.

I want to get on with my life, but I can't, till I hear it straight from him. I need to hear him say hello or goodbye. I need an explanation of where he's been, why he stopped writing and calling, and how he's doing. I hope you can help me find him in some way.

Some Searchers assumed I would charge them for my locator service and were willing to pay me, and others wrote specifically because they thought provided detective searches free of charge. Some writers wanted to know how they could find their Lost Lovers on their own, while others had already tried without success, to find their Lost Lovers, as in this instance:

I HAVE BEEN TRYING TO find [name deleted] for a long time and I have come up empty. We were sweethearts at the University of Wyoming. I believe he came from McDonald, Kansas, but I haven't been able to find anything there either. I sure hope you can help me find him.

Sometimes a change of circumstances, or a need to convey new information to the old flame, triggers a search. One woman wrote extensive details (which have deleted to maintain confidentiality) about the ways she had already tried without success, to find her Lost Lover. She shared this story:

I WAS VERY EXCITED, SURPRISED, and moved by the Lost Love topic on the *Leeza* show. Here's my story: About ten years ago, I met a man in Texas who was either on a student visa, or he could have been a Korean national, or maybe he had dual citizenship. I don't know. We dated for a few years, until I moved away and left no forwarding address for him to contact me. I was avoiding him because of a health condition I had then, that has since cleared, but he had no idea of this and was probably very hurt. He would never call after that because he was too proud and probably afraid of rejection.

Even with all that has happened, I believe that True Love doesn't fade with distance, time, or even death. It stays in the heart forever.

Our love was special. I felt it on a physical and spiritual level, and I believe he did, too. There was so much going on in both of our lives at that time.

I've searched on my own without success. If you could find him I would greatly appreciate it. I enclose additional information that might help.

Some of the Searchers, paralleling the respondents of the Lost Love Project itself, were interested in Lost Lovers whom they met when they were very young, as in this woman's story:

I WAS TEN YEARS OLD when I met the man of my dreams. I spent a year with him, and then he moved away with his family. I've been looking for him ever since. I've gone on with my life and had a child who is now three. I could never fall in love with anyone, though, even though I wanted to, because [name deleted] is the guy of my dreams and has always been in my heart and on my mind.

I desperately want and need to find him, just to know if he is okay, and how life is treating him. When I last saw him, he had brown eyes and brown hair. I have pictured him as looking like Randy on *WKRP in Cincinnati.*

Please help me find him. It's so hard living knowing he's out there somewhere. I love him, always have and probably always will. Thank you. I hope you have better luck than I have.

This writer's stated motivation—just to find out if the Lost Lover is okay, if he is happy—was a prevailing theme through the women's letters. I could not help wondering if they would be satisfied by a letter from the Lost Lover who said, "Hi. Thank you for asking. I'm fine." Probably not! More likely they hope that the Lost Lovers have *not* really been fine without them.

The men, for the most part, stated much more direct motivations for searching, such as this man who wanted to propose marriage:

THE GIRL THAT I WANT to be reunited with is named [name deleted]. She stayed in Oakland, California. She's my first love. I can't seem to locate her. I am still in love with her and would like to marry her. I know that if she sees how good I am doing and that I haven't been in trouble with the law that she would say yes. The only problem is that I can't even afford a ring.

I often have dreams that I have gotten rich somehow and have sent a private detective out to find her so that we could get married and live happily ever after. But I am not rich or even close to it.

If you do decide to help me, it would help me someday get married. Can you tell her that I still love her and I would like to be reunited with her and I finally have an income and my own place. Thanks.

Another man wanted at least to explain his earlier, immature actions:

I WAS HOPING YOU COULD help me find a girl who I was seeing in high school. We haven't seen each other in nine years. I've tried to find her on my own over the last two years but have had no luck.

Her name is [name deleted]. Even though we weren't together very long I fell in love with her. In fact, she was my first love. After a few months together, her family moved away. We continued our relationship long distance and I was supposed to move down with her after the summer. But when the summer ended, I left her instead. I would have been a high school senior, and after talking to my family, I didn't think I was ready to move that far away. To this day, I feel it would have been a mistake, though I regret how I handled the situation. I didn't really explain to her why I was leaving her. We haven't spoken since.

I don't know if she is married or if she has a family, but I would like to find her to tell her how sorry I am for what I did and hopefully we can be friends again. If you could help in any way, I would be very grateful. Otherwise, I don't know what else I can do.

One woman told me she lost track of her Lost Lover right after she turned down his marriage proposal: He wanted to get married that night, but her wedding invitations—to marry a different man—were already in the mail! She said that she wanted to reconnect with him because "He was the only man who ever made my toes curl."

Like some of the participants in the Lost Love Project, many Searchers were still married. One woman in the Midwest gave the following account:

MY HUSBAND IS A GOOD father, *but:* I am so curious about this other person. I have prayed for this fantasy to pass, but it has haunted me over the years.

Would you please help me? The terrible problem is that I can't remember his last name. He was a handsome police officer back east. We saw each other only a few times—I was coming out of a bad relationship and my dad had recently passed away, so the timing wasn't good for me. He was going into the military and he asked for my address. I was very flattered, but I never got around to giving it to him! I have kicked myself royally for that.

I just figured he had so much going for him, I didn't think he was really interested in me. Lately I've thought that if I could just find out where he is, I could get this restless feeling out of my system.

Please reply confidentially!

Another letter from a married woman arrived from Canada, addressed to "Dear Lost Love Helper":

I HAVE BEEN THINKING ABOUT this for about ten years now, quite a bit in the last few. It all started in 1980 when I met the most wonderful man. His name is [name deleted]. I have never met anyone like him again. He was the first guy who took me to a drive-in movie, and the only guy who never pushed me to do something I wasn't ready to do. We spent a summer together.

I still remember the day he left. I was sad but happy to have met such a nice person. We kept in touch for awhile, but lost each other somehow. I think he moved to Alaska.

I have tried all that I know to find him but had no luck. If I could talk with him and ask him how his life is or if he is married I would feel so much better. I am married (two years) and have a wonderful child who keeps most of my time full. But I find myself thinking about him and my mind would be at rest if only I could know how he is doing.

If there is any hope of your telling me how I could go about looking for him *please* call or write. I am hopelessly lost.

And one man demonstrated all the innocence of married respondents in the Lost Love Project who, with their spouses' full approval, "just wanted to have lunch" with their former sweethearts (but who found that the lunch went a little too well):

I'M ONLY TWENTY-FOUR YEARS OLD and have a wife and two wonderful kids, and I'm very happy. I had a beautiful and very charming girlfriend in high school named [name deleted]. Our fathers were both in the military and as dependents we had to go where our fathers had to go. My father had orders to move, so our two years as boyfriend and girlfriend came to an end. It was very hard for both of us to be separated.

We planned to get married in the future, but as the years went by, we lost touch with each other. I think she lives in Texas now, married with one child, but Texas is a big state, and I tried to locate her, without success. I want to see how her life turned out and at least regain our friendship. It's been about seven years since the last time I saw her. It would mean the world to me just to see her face and tell her how happy my life is, and to hope her life has turned out as good as mine.

Sorry for this sloppy letter, but my kids have got me around the neck, so I guess they want to play. P.S. My wife knows I'm writing this letter. Thanks.

My advice to this man's Lost Lover in Texas: If you recognize yourself in this letter, it is best not to make contact with this happily married man (see extra-marital affair statistics, Chapter Six).

I learned from a conversation with Joseph J. Culligan, private investigator and author of *You, Too, Can Find Anybody,* that sometimes Lost Lovers are not really lost at all. They just do not want to be found:

I HAVE A LOST LOVE. I haven't seen him since 1976. I've written to him at least *five times,* without a reply, until a couple days after my birthday in 1992. He promised to call me back, but it's been *two years!!*

I tried calling him but he changed his number a few days after we spoke. Maybe *that* should be telling me *something,* but I still would like to see him again.

His name is [name deleted] and his address is [address deleted], but he has his mail sent to his mother's apartment somewhere in Nevada. I don't know if you can help me to find him but it would be WONDERFUL!! *Please* let me know if you can help me find him.

Some people wanted me to reconnect them with fathers who had left home years ago, children whom they had put up for adoption, or their uncles, cousins, or friends. Ex-wives wrote looking for "deadbeat dads" who were dodging child support payments. A lesbian wrote to tell me that she and her partner were planning to start a family by using artificial insemination, but her partner (who would be the birth mother) did not want a stranger to father their child. This woman wanted me to help locate a dear gay friend of her partner so that she could ask him to be the sperm donor.

Another group of writers asked for relationship advice. One woman sent the following letter:

COULD YOU GIVE ME SOME advice on how to best succeed at a relationship with a man I went to grade school with? I haven't seen this man for a long time, but I recently saw some of his relatives and found out where he worked and that he is single. I called him, and our conversation lasted pretty long, and ended well also. He said he would like me to call him again next time I am in town.

I wanted to ask him to write or call me, but didn't want to be too pushy. I don't know where to go from here. What do you think? I am in my early thirties but not real successful at meeting men my age. Please write back as soon as you can!

Ah, if only I were Dear Abby or Ann Landers! I had to respond by telling her I am not qualified to give such advice. I wonder how her relationship worked out.

After two years of collecting surveys for the Lost Love Project, and of media attention, I received some follow-up mail:

I JUST FINISHED READING AN article about you in our local newspaper. What a surprise to read that you are still doing research on this topic! I wrote to you two years ago after hearing you interviewed on the radio. I asked you to call me, and you did. Now I would like to bring you up to date on the changes in my life.

I finally made the decision to risk a divorce from a husband who loved me deeply and to move to Arizona with my former high school sweetheart. I realized that if I stayed in my marriage, I would be continuing to live a lie. It didn't seem fair to my husband to stay with him while I carried these hidden feelings, and I always would have wondered if my Lost Lover and I could have made a happy life together.

When I did make the move, I had the feeling of "coming home." My feelings of discontent vanished. As soon as my divorce was final, we married. My husband is also very happy and loves to tell the story of how we got back together after thirty-nine years.

It has not always been easy. There are days when I miss my grown children and grandchildren terribly, but I have no regrets. I am so thankful that we can finally live the rest of our lives together.

Keep up the good work. Everyone loves to hear happy love stories, and mine truly has a happy ending.

Some people wrote just to talk about the Lost Love phenomenon with someone who might understand their feelings. One woman sent these insights:

I DEFINITELY BELIEVE THIS IS an important topic. I have yet to find my first love. I keep trying, but at this stage in my life I don't feel that I can locate the party.

During my courtship, my mother played a great part in my not being able to see this person. She even relocated with me, to another city in California, so that he and I would lose contact. Then came World War II and that changed many things in my life.

I have married twice—not too successfully—but I always felt that I had not finished my experience with my first love. There was neither a "Dear John" letter nor an "I don't want to see you."

It is not real satisfying to never feel your life has been completed. I still talk to former male classmates that I knew during grammar school, but it is not the same as finding that old, old love. I do want to thank you for recognizing the problem. Good luck!

And a thank you note arrived from a woman via a Marriott Hotel:

I SAW YOUR PROJECT ON a chat show, and it rang a bell with me. I'm middle aged, married, and living in New Zealand. I often think of and dream about my old high school boyfriend as well as my college boyfriend. Thank you for letting me feel like it's normal.

Yes, it is normal to think or dream about Lost Lovers from high school or college. One man wanted to go a step further: A truck driver wrote to ask me to reconnect him with both his high school and college girlfriends. He's "on the road in different states a lot."

Men also wrote for a sympathetic ear, or to ask about further reading on the topic of rekindled romance, as the following letter illustrates:

MY LOST LOVER [name deleted] was from Tennessee but we met in Illinois. She taught me the meaning of unconditional love; a mid-fifties romance unmatched and never experienced again. We both married, but to others. Now single, I embrace the joy of grandchildren, the fulfillment of a newspaper career long and varied, and peace of mind at trail's end. Yet, for all these years, she remained in my memory mill.

I've always wondered how that first love impacts one's subsequent relationships. In my case, it was profound, and I wonder what you've found in your work. I'd be interested in reading more if you'd point me in the right direction.

One man was worried that an old flame might come back some day:

THE ARTICLE IN *PSYCHOLOGY TODAY* about your work gave me some information about something I've wondered about since divorcing the "love of my life" eight years ago. It's like you read my mind.

I have avoided her like the plague since I left her. She committed adultery, and we had some ugly scenes. But I remember all the good years we had together before this, too. We had that specialness that glorified our intimacy, and I have never had it before or after her. My Rx for avoiding the temptation of sliding back was to go cold turkey from the beginning by not answering her calls and letters, which took seven years to stop! It got so bad I even moved. She stalked me.

I have recently considered getting married again. This wonderful woman has no idea that the power of my former wife still lingers inside me. I can't say that in an ideal situation where my ex came back and promised to live a Christian life with me again, I would stay with my fiancée anyway. I can't say that.

The article about your research confirmed my own suspicions about my feelings. What I *didn't* like to read is that these feelings could ignite ten or more years down the road. I am a Flying Dutchman and I hate it.

Mail also came from my computer information services, such as this correspondence generated by my on-line requests for research participants:

HI, NANCY. I AM A French reporter working for a weekly in Paris. There is another man with the identical name as mine who was at some stage a diplomat, then later a businessman. He seems to have had many a love affair with lots of women who call me, desperately seeking him (I am sorry to say) to try and start up another relationship. The latest woman to call me has not seen him for over 15 years. Interesting?

One letter came from a person of unknown sex, age, and location. The return address simply read "Cupid":

I BELIEVE THAT THE TWO people whose addresses and names I am giving you belong together. They have three children and were young married people who should have stayed together after ten years of marriage and a lot of hard times. All he talks about is her, and all she talks about is him. They are both too stubborn to reconcile! They were married in 1975 and divorced in 1986.

What do you think about a man who *never* stops talking about his ex-wife, and a woman who *never* stops talking about her ex-husband?

Well, good luck!! Here are their names and addresses.

So, do any ex-spouses in New Jersey think Cupid is right?

The most "senior" senior citizen who contacted me about finding a Lost Lover was a woman who wrote from Pennsylvania:

I AM A WIDOW EIGHTY-SEVEN years old. At one time I wrote to Ann Landers about locating my "first love" shall we say?

She suggested high school records, but he quit school. His family moved from our home town in Ohio to another town in Ohio, about 1926. In those days, we had no car and long distance phone calls were unheard of short of death! He could have written, but let me go.

I have never really forgotten him, even though I was married forty-eight years. I am curious to know his whereabouts, or if he is deceased. Then I can put him to rest in my heart. I do not want to disturb his present life (or wife!). His name is [name deleted], though I am unsure of the spelling. Thank you for your assistance.

The youngest person to mail a letter to me about a Lost Love search was a girl in Nevada. She printed in pencil, on lined paper torn from a spiral notebook:

HI. MY NAME IS [name deleted]. I'm twelve years old and boy do I have a story too tell you! It begins in the summer of 1990.

I was going to go and visit my twenty-seven year old sister. I met this girl who is now my best friend. She was eight. She had a boyfriend and his best friend was [name deleted]. He was twelve. I was only nine at the time. Oh ya by the way my sister lived in Maryland in an apt. complex that had a pool. You have to be twelve to be able to swim without an adult. Iv been swimming by myself since I was three years old. And even tho I was only nine people thought I was around twelve, so my sister said just to tell everbody that I was twelve so she wouldn't have to watch me.

But eny way I told everybody so only my best friend new my real age. Well, one day we were at the pool and two boys came down. When I'm around really cute boys I run away because I'm really shy. But after a wile I got to know them better so I said I would go skating with them and her. [name deleted] had one of those smiles that could melt a girl's heart. I may have only been nine years old, but a lot of people say age don't matter it's the love that you have for them. He thought I was twelve so he asked me out.

And so the rest of the summer was awsome. But when it was

time to go back home to Hawaii, all of my friends planed a going away party and my friend's mom made a card and everbody signed it. [name deleted] said he was going to give me my special surprise present (I thought he was going to give me a ring or something like that). He gave me 80 dollors to spend on what ever. But it's been almost four years since Iv seen him. He moved. We had such a fun time over there. I just wish we can get back together and this time I hope it's forever. I just want to at least hear his voice again. That would be so great.

Do you think you could try to put us back together? Please please please. I'll do enything please you don't know how much he means to me! If you can put us back together I would do eny favors that you need done. Please he means so much to me. I belive you can bring us back together—I have a lot of faith and trust. Thanks a lot! Love [name deleted]

If my young correspondent should by some chance see this, I would like her to know that I think I do know how much he means to her. I have heard from more than 1,001 people from all over the world, and many of them were about her age when they first met the true love they would reconnect with permanently and passionately so many years later. She is indeed right that age doesn't matter if the love is real. I wish her good luck in her search.

I tried to remember the names of the Searchers and the Lost Lovers as I read through the many letters. It would have been wonderful to discover a match. But I never did. So many people, of all ages and from all walks of life, seek the comfort of a familiar love, a true love, and I had the privilege of hearing from only a fraction of them.

My youngest correspondent wrote to me via e-mail in a Romance Forum, in response to my posted request for new Lost Love Project participants:

HI. IM EIGHT YEARS OLD. I know Im young but Im still RO-MANTIC. Im surching for my true love.

I understand. I am still searching, too. My own rekindled romance did not work out in the end. But that experience led to this fascinating project, which changed my life in substantial and wonderful ways. Happy endings sometimes take a different form than we imagine, but they are just as happy. So despite my own Lost and Found and Lost Again Love story, I always encourage others to follow their hearts and contact the Lost Lovers who still haunt their dreams.

Is there someone out there whom you knew and loved years ago, waiting for *you* to call? I wish you the very special gifts of Lost and Found Love.

POSTSCRIPT

HOW TO PARTICIPATE IN THE LOST LOVE PROJECT

Did you love someone years ago, part, then five or more years later try another relationship with that person? Would you like to become involved in the continuation of the Lost Love Project?

Or, if you have already participated, would you like to share an update of your Lost Love story? Do you have any insights to add to those in this book?

Are you a relative or friend or ex-spouse of a rekindler who would like to share your perspective on renewed love? Are you a practicing therapist who has some thoughts to add about Lost and Found Lovers as clients? Or are you a private investigator who would like to share your experiences finding Lost Lovers?

I would like to hear from you. Please write to me at:

Lost Love Project

P.O. Box 19692

Sacramento, CA 95819

Or you may contact me on-line at **74537.1114@compuserve.com.** or at **nkalish@csus.edu**

Watch for a World Wide Web page, coming soon!

APPENDIX I

THE LOST AND FOUND LOVE HIT PARADE

Again . . . . .Janet Jackson

Back in My Arms Again . . . . .The Supremes

Book of Love . . . . .The Monotones

Come in out of the Rain . . . . .Windy Moten

Coming Back to Me . . . . .Jefferson Airplane

Escape (The Piña Colada Song) . . . . .Reupert Holmes

Falling Out of Love . . . . .Reba McEntire

Here Come Those Tears Again .Jackson Browne

Here You Come Again . . . . .Dolly Parton

I Started Loving You Again . . . . .Barbara Mandrell

I'll Never Say 'Never Again' Again . . . . .Harry MacGregor Woods

It Started All Over Again . . . . .Tommy Dorsey; Frank Sinatra

It's Been a Long, Long Time . . . . .Sammy Cahn and Jules Styne

Martha . . . . .Tom Waits

Mathilde . . . . .Jacques Brel

Never Can Say Good-bye . . . . .Jackson Five

Never Gonna Let You Go . . . . .Joe Pizzulo and Lisa Miller

New Looks from an Old Lover .B J Thomas

Now You Tell Me . . . . .Reba McEntire

Old Flame . . . . .Alabama

One More Try . . . . .George Michael

One Promise Too Late . . . . .Reba McEntire

Reunion . . . . .Erasure

Reunited . . . . .Peaches and Herb

Same Old Lang Syne . . . . .Dan Fogelberg

Same Old Walk . . . . .Paul Kelly

Second Time Around . . . . .Frank Sinatra

Send in the Clowns . . . . .Stephen Sondheim

Tie a Yellow Ribbon . . . . .Tony Orlando and Dawn

Too Many Mornings . . . . .Stephen Sondheim

Unanswered Prayers . . . . .Garth Brooks

What Kind of Fool . . . . .Barbra Streisand and Barry Gibb

You Keep Coming Back . . . . .Richard Marx

APPENDIX II

THE LOST LOVE PROJECT PARTICIPANTS

CURRENT ADDRESSES BY STATE AND COUNTRY

AK 2	MA 14	OR 25	Brazil 1	Israel 4
AL 17	MD 22	PA 43	Canada:	Italy 2
AR 8	ME 2	RI 22	AB 4	Japan 3
AZ 20	MI 55	SC 13	BC 21	Malaysia 3
CA 156	MN 14	SD 4	NB 1	Netherlands 3
CO 67	MO 9	TN 15	ON 29	New Zealand 4
CT 19	MS 11	TX 54	QE 6	Philippines 1
DE 1	MT 4	UT 9	Chile 2	Russia 1
FL 76	NC 21	VA 16	Czech Rep. 1	Scotland 4
GA 11	ND 2	VT 5	Denmark 1	Singapore 1
HI 22	NE 8	WA 42	Ecuador 1	Slovak Rep. 1
IA 10	NH 4	WI 15	Egypt 1	South Africa 4
ID 1	NJ 51	WV 5	England 13	Spain 1
IL 105	NM 10	WY 2	France 5	Sweden 2
IN 18	NV 9	Wash, D.C. 4	Germany 4	Switzerland 4
KS 3	NY 48	Puerto Rico 3	Hong Kong 2	Thailand 1
KY 8	OH 23	Argentina 1	India 1	Venezuela 1
LA 7	OK 15	Australia 9	Ireland 2	

(1,001 questionnaire participants, and 294 participants with stories only)

The Lost Love Project sampled the participants only once, so there is no way to know how many of those couples who checked "We Are Still Together" were still together even one day after the survey was completed, or are still together now. There is no way to know how many who checked "We Are Engaged" will actually marry. Some who checked "We Have No Contact" might become rekindled lovers again some day. However, since these people reunited with their former sweethearts at any time prior to filling out the survey—from just recently to more than fifty years ago—there is a built-in follow-up.

Further, this is not a random sample. There is no ethical way to take a group of men and women and randomly assign only half of them to rekindle a romance, while the other half would not. The Lost Love Project respondents were self-selected rekindlers, and there is no control group of nonrekindlers to whom to compare them.

It is not even possible to know if the people who contributed to the Lost Love Project are typical of rekindlers as a whole. These people, in addition to rekindling a romance after five or more years, saw the ad for the Lost Love Project; had enough motivation to request participation, fill out the questionnaire, and return it; and—if not native English speakers—knew English well enough to understand the ad and the survey questions.

For all these reasons, conclusions can be drawn only for these participants in the Lost Love Project, and not for all the Lost and Found Lovers of the world.

On the following pages is the questionnaire that was mailed to all the Lost Love Project participants. The percentages that indicate how many people chose each response are given in parentheses. Some people did not answer certain questions, and some people answered with more than one choice, so percentages do not necessarily total 100%.

Tests for significance levels were the analysis of variance and chi square, at $p < .01$. This means that when the terms "significant" and "statistically significant" are used in the text, it indicates that the results could have occurred by chance only less than once out of 100 events.

LOST LOVE EXPERIENCE QUESTIONNAIRE

(WITH RESULTS ADDED)

If you have renewed love relationships with more than one Lost Lover, please answer the following questions as they apply to the renewed relationship that was MOST IMPORTANT TO YOU.

1. How many times in your life have you renewed relationships with various Lost Lovers? (check one)

%

(82) ☐ 1

(13) ☐ 2

(3) ☐ 3

(1) ☐ 4

(1) ☐ More than 4

2. How old were you and your Lost Lover when you began your relationship the first time? (check answers)

%	You	Lost Lover		
(55)	☐	☐	**(46)**	17 or younger
(29)	☐	☐	**(35)**	18 to 22
(10)	☐	☐	**(12)**	23 to 29
(4)	☐	☐	**(5)**	30 to 39
(2)	☐	☐	**(2)**	40 or over

3. How long did your original relationship last? (check one)

%

(3) ☐ 1 month

(14) ☐ 2 to 6 months

(19) ☐ 7 to 12 months

(37) ☐ 13 months to 3 years

(15) ☐ 4 to 5 years

(12) ☐ Over 5 years

4. Was this person your first love? (check one)

%

(62) ☐ Yes

(38) ☐ No

5. Which of the following would characterize your original relationship? (check all that apply)

%

(46) ☐ Dated each other without being sexually involved

(48) ☐ Dated each other with sexual involvement

(7) ☐ Lived together

(10) ☐ Became engaged

(6) ☐ Married

6. Who left the original relationship? (check one)

%

(41) ☐ You

(35) ☐ Lost Lover

(23) ☐ Mutual agreement

7. What was the PRIMARY reason for one or both of you that you separated? (check one)

%

(11) ☐ Too young

(0.1) ☐ Sexually incompatible

(11) ☐ Moved away

(7) ☐ Left to attend school

(9) ☐ Didn't want to make a commitment

(3) ☐ Not getting along well

(25) ☐ Parents disapproved

(0.6) ☐ No common interests

(13) ☐ Began dating someone else

(7) ☐ Had different expectations

(5) ☐ Lived too far apart

(0) ☐ Children disapproved

(5) ☐ Couldn't leave a marriage or significant other

(8) ☐ Other _____

8. If there was parental disapproval, what was the disapproval based on? (check one)

%

(6) ☐ Parent(s) did not like the person's personality

(3) ☐ We were different races

(3) ☐ We had different religions

(0.7) ☐ We were from different ethnic groups

(2) ☐ We were from different socioeconomic groups

(2) ☐ The age difference between us bothered parents

(6) ☐ Parent(s) thought we were too young

(3) ☐ Fear of our sexual involvement

9. After you separated, how long did it take you to recover emotionally from this separation? (check one)

%

(9) ☐ Less than 1 month

(21) ☐ 2 to 5 months

(18) ☐ 6 to 12 months

(21) ☐ 13 months to 3 years

(7) ☐ 4 to 5 years

(6) ☐ 6 to 10 years

(17) ☐ Over 10 years

The following questions refer to your renewed relationship with your Lost Lover after being separated for 5 or more years:

10. Who initiated the renewal of the relationship? (check one)

%

(41) ☐ I

(33) ☐ Lost Lover

(25) ☐ It was mutual

11. How did you find each other again? (check one)

%

(10) ☐ Bumped into each other by chance

(6) ☐ Saw each other at a school reunion

(13) ☐ I wrote to Lost Lover

(8) ☐ Lost Lover wrote to me

(21) ☐ I telephoned Lost Lover

(18) ☐ Lost Lover telephoned me

(20) ☐ Through a friend or relative

(2) ☐ Heard about Lost Lover through radio, TV, newspaper

12. How long had it been since you had been in contact with your Lost Lover? (check one)

%

(34) ☐ 5 to 10 years

(17) ☐ 11 to 15 years

(12) ☐ 16 to 20 years

(11) ☐ 21 to 25 years

(10) ☐ 26 to 30 years

(6) ☐ 31 to 35 years

(10) ☐ 36 to 40 years

(0.8) ☐ Over 40 years

13. How much time passed between the time you contacted or met with your Lost Lover again and the time you resumed a relationship? (check one)

%

(24) ☐ less than 1 week

(24) ☐ 1 to 3 weeks

(29) ☐ 1 to 6 months

(10) ☐ 7 months to 1 year

(12) ☐ More than a year

14. How long did your renewed relationship with Lost Lover last?

%

(2) ☐ Only 1 meeting

(2) ☐ Less than 1 week

(3) ☐ 1 month

(6) ☐ 2 to 6 months

(4) ☐ 7 to 12 months

(6) ☐ 13 months to 3 years

(3) ☐ 4 to 5 years

(2) ☐ More than 5 years

(72) ☐ We're still together

15. What was your marital status at the time of your renewed relationship? (check one)

%

(20) ☐ Single

(3) ☐ Living with significant other

(1) ☐ Engaged

(30) ☐ Married

(11) ☐ Separated

(28) ☐ Divorced

(7) ☐ Widowed

16. What was the distance between your residence and your Lost Lover's residence when you renewed your relationship? (check one)

%

(15) ☐ 1 to 10 miles

(13) ☐ 11 to 50 miles

(8) ☐ 51 to 100 miles

(17) ☐ 101 to 500 miles

(11) ☐ 501 to 1,000 miles

(36) ☐ More than 1,000 miles

For questions number 17 to 19 only, using a scale of 1 to 5, with 5 being the MOST and 1 being the LEAST, please rate the following:

17. How FAST did your renewed relationship proceed compared to other relationships you have had in the past?

	1	2	3	4	5
%	**(6)**	**(6)**	**(12)**	**(15)**	**(61)**

18. How would you describe your EMOTIONAL involvement in your renewed relationship compared to that in other relationships you have had in the past? (circle one)

1 ....2 ....3 ....4 5

%	(4)	(4)	(8)	(13)	(71)

19. How INTENSE was your SEXUAL involvement in your renewed relationship with Lost Lover compared to that in other relationships you have had in the past? (circle one)

1 ....2 ....3 ....4 5

%	(10)	(6)	(7)	(11)	(63)

20. Were there any things that you saved from your original relationship? Did you share any of these things with your Lost Lover? (check all that apply)

Saved	Shared	
%	%	
(47) ☐	(38) ☐	Letters, poems, or cards written from one of you
(43) ☐	(31) ☐	Gifts from Lost Lover
(68) ☐	(57) ☐	Photographs of one or both of you
(42) ☐	(35) ☐	Souvenirs/memorabilia of the times you spent together
(35) ☐	(39) ☐	Old records/music from the time you spent together

21. In your renewed relationship with your Lost Lover, did you (check all that apply):

%

(71) ☐ Think about Lost Lover constantly

(61) ☐ Spend excessive time on the telephone with Lost Lover

(32) ☐ Spend excessive money on visits/activities

(18) ☐ Become jealous of time spent apart

(46) ☐ Spend a lot of time writing letters to Lost Lover

(35) ☐ Spend a lot of time together

(19) ☐ Purchase a lot of gifts for each other

(50) ☐ Travel frequently to see each other

(29) ☐ Have trouble eating and/or sleeping

(24) ☐ Send each other recordings of old music

(15) ☐ Use Express Mail or overnight delivery because regular mail was too slow

22. If you renewed your relationship with Lost Lover, did you (check all that apply):

%

(25) ☐ Date each other without being sexually involved

(69) ☐ Date each other with sexual involvement

(30) ☐ Live together

(30) ☐ Become engaged

(33) ☐ Marry

(1.5) ☐ Divorce

23. Would you describe the renewed relationship as being worthwhile for any of the following reasons? (check all that apply)

%

(43) ☐ Gave us a chance to make amends

(34) ☐ Got to hear why he/she left

(44) ☐ Felt better about our past together after talking about it

(32) ☐ Finally able to free myself from a recurring fantasy of Lost Lover

(47) ☐ Realized that relationship could not have worked then

(57) ☐ Got to recapture the past/old parts of myself

(49) ☐ Felt young again

24. If your renewed relationship with Lost Lover ended, what do you consider the PRIMARY reason it ended? (check one)

%

(0) ☐ We were too young

(0.3) ☐ We were sexually incompatible

(1) ☐ One of us moved away

(1) ☐ One of us wanted commitment and the other did not

(0.6) ☐ We were not getting along well

(0.2) ☐ Parents disapproved

(2) ☐ One of us began dating someone else

(0) ☐ We didn't have common interests

(3) ☐ Lost Lover passed away

(3) ☐ We had different expectations

(0.9) ☐ We lived too far apart

(2) ☐ Children disapproved

(5) ☐ One of us couldn't leave a marriage or significant other

(1) ☐ One of us couldn't leave a job

(2) ☐ Differences in values

(72) ☐ Not applicable (we are still together)

(4) ☐ Other _____

25. If your renewed relationship ended, did you spend time recovering from this loss? If so, how long? (check one)

%

(7) ☐ Less than 1 month

(2) ☐ 1 month

(6) ☐ 2 to 6 months

(2) ☐ 7 to 12 months

(4) ☐ 1 to 3 years

(6) ☐ Over 3 years

(72) ☐ Not applicable (we are still together)

26. If you could renew your relationship with your Lost Lover again, would you? (check one)

%

(53) ☐ Yes

(24) ☐ No

(10) ☐ I'm not sure

27. What is your relationship to your Lost Lover now? (check one)

%

(14) ☐ We have no contact

(9) ☐ We write or call, but do not see each other

(8) ☐ We are friends but not sexually involved

(21) ☐ We are lovers

(7) ☐ We live together

(7) ☐ We are engaged

(30) ☐ We are married

(1.5) ☐ We are separated or divorced

(3) ☐ He/she is deceased

28. At this point in time, if you are separated from your Lost Lover, does it feel like your relationship is permanently over? (check one)

%

(14) ☐ Yes

(53) ☐ No

(11) ☐ I'm not sure

%   **(33)**   **(67)**

29. You are: ☐ Male   ☐ Female

Your Lost Lover is: ☐ Male   ☐ Female

%   **(67)**   **(33)**

30. Your current marital status is (check one):

%

  (9) ☐ Single, never married

  (5) ☐ Living with significant other

  (4) ☐ Engaged

(47) ☐ Married

  (6) ☐ Separated but not divorced

(24) ☐ Divorced

  (6) ☐ Widowed

31. Your highest level of education is (check one):

%

(0.2) ☐ Junior high or less

  (3) ☐ Some high school

  (9) ☐ High school graduate

(30) ☐ Some college

(26) ☐ College graduate

(32) ☐ Graduate or professional school after college

32. Your household income is (check one):

%

(4) ☐ Under 10,000

(7) ☐ 10,000 to 19,000

(24) ☐ 20,000 to 39,000

(25) ☐ 40,000 to 59,000

(17) ☐ 60,000 to 79,000

(21) ☐ 80,000 or more

33. In what year were you born? _____

If you would like to provide more detailed information about this relationship, please feel free to use the space provided below or attach additional sheets if necessary.

Thank you!

REFERENCES

Andersen, Hans Christian. (1991) *Fairytales*. Translated by L. W. Kingsland. New York: Oxford University Press.

Ansberry, Clare. (1994) First love, second time around. *Good Housekeeping*. July, 48–52.

Berger, Kathleen Stassen. (1991) *The developing person through childhood and adolescence*. New York: Worth Publishers.

Bettelheim, Bruno. (1976) *The uses of enchantment*. New York: Alfred A. Knopf.

Biddle, Julian. (1994) *What was hot*. New York: Windsor Press.

Bilicki, Bettie Youngs, and Goetz, Masa. (1990) *Getting back together*. MA: Bob Adams.

Bioletti, Harry L. (1989) *The yanks are coming: the American invasion of New Zealand 1942–1944*. Auckland: Century Hutchinson.

Brontë, Charlotte. (1981) *Jane Eyre*. New York: Bantam Books.

Brooks, Tim, and Marsh, Earle. (1992) *The complete directory to prime time network TV shows 1946–present*. New York: Ballantine Books.

Capellanus, Andreas. (1964) *The art of courtly love*. New York: Frederick Ungar Publishing Co.

Clark, Leslie F., and Collins, James E. (1993) Remembering old flames: how the past affects assessments of the present. *Personality and Social Psychology Bulletin, 19*, 339–408.

Collins, James E., and Clark, Leslie F. (1989) Responsibility and rumination: the trouble with understanding the dissolution of a relationship. *Social Cognition, 7*, 152–173.

Culligan, Joseph J. (1994) *You, too, can find anybody*. Hallmark Press.

DiGaetani, John Louis. (1986) *An invitation to the opera*. New York: Doubleday.

DiMartino, Dave. (1994) *Hit billboard makers' singer-songwriters*. New York: Billboard Books.

Dutton, D., and Aron, A. (1974) Some evidence for heightened sexual attraction under conditions of high anxiety. *Journal of Personality and Social Psychology, 30*, 510–517.

Ebert, Roger. (1989) *Roger Ebert's movie home companion*. Kansas City: Andrews and McMeel.

Elkind, David. (1974) *Children and adolescents: interpretive essays on Jean Piaget*. New York: Oxford University Press.

Fishbein, Ed. (1995) Garcia's heirs not all grateful. *The Sacramento Bee,* December 3, A2.

Fitzgerald, F. Scott. (1992) *The great Gatsby.* New York: Collier.

Foreman, Michael. (1991) *World of fairytales.* New York: Arcade Publishing.

Fowler, Will, and Jacques, Hal. (1994) The star-crossed marriage of Marilyn and Joe. *Remember.* August/September.

Freeman, John W. (1984) *The Metropolitan Opera stories of the great operas.* New York: W. W. Norton.

Gabe, Grace. (1993) Rekindling old flames. *Psychology Today.* September/October, 32–39, 62–63.

Gassner, John (editor). (1963) *A treasury of the theatre.* New York: Simon and Schuster.

Genesis 25.1. (1978) Brooklyn: Mesurah Publishing, Ltd.

Gould, R. L. (1978) *Transformations: Growth and change in adult life.* New York: Simon and Schuster.

Halpern, Howard M. (1983) *How to break your addiction to a person.* New York: Bantam Books.

Halpern, Paul. (1990) *Time journeys.* New York: McGraw-Hill.

Harris, Blase. (1989) *How to get your lover back.* New York: Dell Publishing.

Havighurst, R. J. (1952) *Developmental tasks and education.* New York: McKay.

Jacobs, Dick, and Jacobs, Harriett. (1994) *Who wrote that song?* Cincinnati: Writers Digest Books.

Johnson, Robert A. (1983) *We.* New York: Harper and Row.

Keillor, Garrison. (1987) *Leaving home.* New York: Viking Penguin, Inc.

Leroux, Gaston. (1987) *The phantom of the opera.* New York: Harper and Row.

Levinson, D. J. (1978) *The seasons of a man's life.* New York: Knopf.

Levy, Newman. (1958) *The Rodgers and Hammerstein song book.* New York: Simon and Schuster.

Lodge, David. (1995) *Therapy.* New York: Viking.

Márquez, Gabriel García. (1989) *Love in the time of cholera.* New York: Penguin Books.

Norwood, Robin. (1985) *Women who love too much.* Los Angeles: Jeremy P. Tarcher.

Ogden, Christopher. (1994) *The life of the party.* New York: Little, Brown, and Company.

Olds, Sally Wendkos. (1985) *The eternal garden.* New York: Times Books.

Panati, Charles. (1991) *Parade of fads, follies, and manias.* New York: HarperCollins.

Phillips-Matz, M. (1993) *Verdi: a biography.* New York: Oxford University Press.

Rawlins, William K. (1992) *Friendship matters: communication, dialectics, and the life course.* New York: Aldine De Gruyter.

Rice, F. Philip. (1987) *The adolescent.* Newton: Allyn and Bacon, Inc.

Riley, James Whitcomb. (1910) *The girl I loved.* New York: Bobbs-Merrill Co.

Rodgers, Richard, and Hart, Lorenz. (1984) *Rodgers and Hart: a musical anthology.* Milwaukee: Hal Leonard Publishing Corporation.

Rosenthal, Robert, and Rosnow, Ralph L. (1969) *Artifact in behavioral research.* New York: Academic Press.

Santrock, John W. (1983) *Life-span development.* Dubuque: Wm. C. Brown Co.

Shea, Laurie; Thompson, Linda; and Blieszner, Rosemary. (1988) Resources in older adults' old and new friendships. *Journal of Social and Personal Relationships, 5,* 83–96.

Shreve, Anita. (1993) *Where or when.* New York: Harcourt Brace.

Simon, George T. (1981) *The big bands song book.* New York: HarperCollins.

Simpson, Eileen. (1994) *Late love.* New York: Houghton Mifflin.

Smelser, Neil J., and Erikson, Erik H. (1980) *Themes of work and love in adulthood.* Cambridge: Harvard University Press.

Waller, Niels G., and Shaver, Phillip R. (1994) The importance of nongenetic influences on romantic love styles: a twin-family study. *Psychological Science, 5,* 268–273.

Waller, Robert James. (1992) *The bridges of Madison County.* New York: Warner Books.

Willens, Michelle. (1994) Lost loves reignited and reunited. *The New York Times.* February 10, C1.

INDEX

Johnson, Martin A., 24–25
Johnson, Robert A., 69
Johnston, Arthur James, 179
J. Peterman clothing catalogue, 57

Keaton, Diane, 61
Keillor, Garrison, 61
Kern, Jerome, 79
KFBK, 2

Late adulthood, 10, 113–117, 147–149, 181
    acceptance of mortality during, 114
    illness during, 115, 116
lawsuits, custody, 27
Leeza, 4, 8, 181, 186
Levinson, Daniel, 105
Life of the Party, The (Ogden), 60
Lodge, David, 75
long-distance relationships, 150, 188
Longevity, 154
lost and found children, 21–22, 191
lost and found lovers:
    as action-oriented, 48
    anger of, 50, 59–60, 75, 116, 167, 173–174
    capacity for forgiveness by, 50
    career conflicts of, 172
    characteristics of, 45–51, 146–147, 148, 152,
        165–166
    children from previous marriages of, 26, 27–29,
        131, 143, 151, 159, 160, 162, 164
    children of, 21–22, 79, 84, 162
    demographics of, 11–15
    desire to talk of, 7–8, 18, 45
    and dysfunction of prior marriages, 40, 92,
        164
    emotional health of, 22–23
    famous, 58–65
    health challenges and, 36, 76–77, 115–116,
        123, 126, 152, 155, 162, 163
    homosexuality and, 12, 40, 171
    how reunited, 141–148
    mental illness and, 40–41
    neediness of, 50
    optimism of, 48, 82, 121, 148
    as risk takers, 48, 143, 148
    romantic traits of, 48–49, 148, 152
    shared background of, 34–36, 41–42, 70
    spirituality of, 47, 50, 155, 164
    spouses of, 27–28, 158, 161, 162, 163, 164,
        167, 171, 190

widows and widowers as, 3, 11, 28, 48, 148,
        157, 163, 172
    see also rekindled romances
lost friends, 191
Lost Love Project, 18, 20, 24, 30, 35, 46, 47, 48,
        49, 50, 52, 54, 58, 59, 60, 71, 72, 73,
        76, 80, 81, 84, 89, 91, 93, 95, 100, 103,
        104, 106, 119, 120, 122, 134, 142, 143,
        147, 149, 150, 152, 156, 157, 164, 165,
        175, 176, 177, 179, 181, 187, 189, 190,
        197
    as creating rekindled romances, 5–6
    international aspect of, 3, 4, 5, 13–14
    and media, 1, 2–3, 4–6, 8, 180, 192
    methodology of, 205
    participation in, 199
    questionnaire, 1, 2, 6, 7, 11, 13, 208–217
lost lovers:
    as "back-up plan," 183
    desire to avoid, 194
    methods of locating, 180
    nameless, 180, 189
    unfound, 179–191, 193, 195–197
    yearning for, 183
lost love searches, 22–23, 47–48
    by married searchers, 189–190
    methods of conducting, 180
    motivations for, 181, 182, 184–185, 187–188,
        193
    obstacles to, 121
lost parents, 191
love:
    courtly, 66, 70, 73, 101, 165
    deepened by suffering, 73
    definition of, 54
Love Among the Ruins, 84
Love in the Time of Cholera (García Márquez), 73, 75
lovers:
    idealization of, 70
    "impaired," 51–52
    jealousy of, 53–54, 60, 66, 67, 75
love styles, attitude and preferences about, 36
love tokens, 67, 152–153, 170, 185

Madame Butterfly (Puccini), 77
marriage/divorce/rematch pattern, 59, 65, 116,
        124, 169
married lovers, 9–10, 18–19, 23, 31–32, 40, 45,
        54, 152, 156–157, 171, 181
Marriott Hotels, 57, 193
Meier, Barbara, 58

as healing mechanism, 80, 119, 145
school, 8, 11, 24, 83, 142
reunited divorced couples, 19, 54–55, 124–125
    see also marriage/divorce/rematch pattern
reunited first loves, 10–11, 19, 31, 121–122, 143,
        172, 175
reunited high school sweethearts, 8, 11, 19, 28,
        39, 41, 54–55, 57, 58–59, 136, 142, 173,
        181, 192
reversibility, 95
Riley, James Whitcomb, 73
Ritter, Malcolm, 6
romances:
    destructive, 51–52, 54
    new, 33–34, 149
    office, 53
Roosevelt, Edith, 62–63
Roosevelt, Eleanor, 64
Roosevelt, Franklin, 64
Roosevelt, Theodore, 63

Scarlett, 84
Schmidt, Harvey, 81
school reunions, 8, 11, 24, 83, 142
Seasons of a Man's Life, The (Levinson), 105
second breakups:
    grieving after, 170–171
    reasons for, 171–173
    see also rekindled romance, failures of
self-esteem, 22–23
separation anxiety, 89, 91, 93
serial monogamy, 51–52
sexual abuse, 38
sexual harassment, 33
Shakespeare, William, 69
Shaver, Phillip R., 36
Shea, Laurie, 35
Show Boat (Kern and Hammerstein), 79
Shreve, Anita, 75
Simpson, Nicole, 60
Simpson, O. J., 60
Sisters, 85
soap operas, 84
songs, 85, 201

stagnation, generativity vs., 105
Stars and Stripes, 18
step-siblings, 28–29
Stolz, Teresa, 58
stranger anxiety, 88, 91, 93
Strepponi, Giuseppina, 58
suicide, 53, 77, 78
Sullivan Street Playhouse, 81

Talk shows, 2, 4, 5, 8, 19, 24, 84, 146, 180
Taylor, Elizabeth, 59
teenage pregnancy, 21
Therapy (Lodge), 75
Thompson, Linda, 35
tokens of love, 67, 152–153, 170, 185
Tom Sullivan Show, The, 2
Transformations: Growth and Change in Adult Life
        (Gould), 105
Traviata, La (Verdi), 58
Tristan and Iseult, 66–68
    Iseult the Fair as anima in, 69, 71
Tristan und Isolde (Wagner), 78
"12 Step Amends," 120

Verdi, Giuseppe, 58
Vietnam War, 12, 21, 39–40, 68, 184

Wagner, Richard, 78
Waller, Niels G., 36
Waller, Robert James, 1
We (Johnson), 69
Wesendonck, Mathilde, 78
Where or When (Shreve), 75
widows, widowers, 3, 11, 28, 48, 148, 157, 163,
        172, 182, 195
Wolfe, Thomas, 47
World War II, 3, 60, 76, 129, 132, 134, 143,
        163, 181, 193

Yanks Are Coming, The (Bioletti), 129
You, Too, Can Find Anybody (Culligan), 191